AF608687

**Randgänge der Mediävistik**

Edited by Michael Stolz

**Volume 11**

JEFFREY F. HAMBURGER

# Spaces of Knowledge in Medieval Diagrams

Schwabe Verlag

The Deutsche Nationalbibliothek lists this publication in the Deutsche Nationalbibliografie; detailed bibliographic data are available on the Internet at http://dnb.dnb.de.


Cover design: icona basel gmbH, Basel
Cover: Kathrin Strohschnieder, stroh design, Oldenburg
Copy editing: Kate Bird, Berlin
Typesetting: Daniela Weiland, textformart, Göttingen
Print: Beltz Grafische Betriebe GmbH, Bad Langensalza
Printed in Germany
Manufacturer information: Schwabe Verlagsgruppe AG, St. Alban-Vorstadt 76, 4052 Basel, info@schwabeverlag.ch
Responsible person under Art. 16 GPSR: Schwabe Verlag GmbH, Marienstraße 28, 10117 Berlin, info@schwabeverlag.de
ISBN Print 978-3-7965-5411-7
ISBN e-Book (PDF) 978-3-7965-5412-4
DOI 10.24894/978-3-7965-5412-4
The e-Book has identical page numbers to the print edition (first printing) and supports full-text search. Furthermore, the table of contents is linked to the headings.

rights@schwabe.ch
www.schwabe.ch

Contents

7 **Defining the Diagram**
11 **From Plato to Peirce**
17 **The Scene of the Diagram**
21 **The Divided Line**
25 **Dimensions of Diairesis in the Pseudo-Dionysius**
43 **Figures of Thought**
53 **The Athletic Scholar**
63 **About the Author**

# Defining the Diagram

Diagrams present a special instance of the figure-ground relationship, which is as central to cognition as it is to the visual arts.[1] In architectural and urban studies, a figure-ground diagram charts the relationship between built and unbuilt spaces. Built spaces are normally shown in black (or some other color); streets are left blank. Neither is more important than the other; each connotes a different category of information. Other images exploit the figure-ground relationship to create what are called bistable images, which in turn are linked to perceptual multistability, the coexistence of two mutually exclusive perceptual states. Of this type of image, perhaps the most familiar are Edgar Rubin's vase, in which one perceives either a black vase against a white background or a pair of white faces on a black background, and Joseph Jastrow's rabbit/duck made famous by Wittgenstein's 'Philosophical Investigations', in which he used it to distinguish "seeing that" from "seeing as", ordinary perception as opposed to seeing under an aspect.[2]

In ancient and medieval Greek, the word *διάγραμμα* (*diágramma*) derives from the verb *διαγράφειν*, "to mark out by lines". Diagrams conventionally consist of lines drawn on a blank background, whether of parchment or paper, although they can, of course, subsist in other media, whether dust on the ground (as in Valerius Maximus's apocryphal account of the death of Archimedes) or the virtual space

**1** This essay draws to a significant extent on portions of my book, Jeffrey F. Hamburger, The Areopagite through The Ages. A Millennium of Diagramming the Pseudo-Dionysius, c. 600–c. 1600. Toronto forthcoming. I am grateful to Michael Stolz for providing me with an opportunity to expand on some its ideas here, to Eva Schlotheuber for bringing my text to his attention, to Herbert Kessler for a close reading, and to John Kee for his assistance in transcribing and translating Greek inscriptions. Any errors remain my own.

**2** See Jörgen L. Pind, Edgar Rubin and Psychology in Denmark. Figure and Ground (History and Philosophy of Psychology). Cham 2014. From the enormous literature on Wittgenstein, I cite only William James Earle, Ducks and Rabbits. Visuality in Wittgenstein. In: David M. Kleinberg-Levin (ed.), Sites of Vision: The Discursive Construction of Sight in the History of Philosophy. Cambridge MA 1999, pp. 293–314; and Emmanuel Alloa, Seeing-as, Seeing-in, Seeing-with: Looking Through Images. In: Richard Heinrich et al. (eds.), Image and Imaging in Philosophy, Science and the Arts. Proceedings of the 33rd International Ludwig Wittgenstein Symposium in Kirchberg, 2010, 2 vols. (Image and Imagining in Philosophy, Science and the Arts 1; Publications of the Austrian Ludwig Wittengenstein Society, NS 16). Berlin 2011, vol. 1, pp. 179–190.

of a computer screen.[3] They consist, however, of more than lines alone. The lines serve as outlines, that is, they surround or subtend an area of a particular shape.[4] Even if they are colored, they still have contours.[5] This duality of line and plane poses a series of questions: when looking at a diagram, do the lines command our attention? Or rather the spaces those lines enclose? Are the lines contours demarcating spaces and denoting limits? Or are they the connective tissue within a network of nodes, as in graph theory? In either case, the answer is both, albeit to variable degrees depending on content and context.

Another way of posing these questions is to ask whether diagrams are inherently spatial. The Euclidean proof of the Pythagorean theorem offers an instructive example: the sum of the areas of the two squares on the legs of a right triangle equals the area of the square on the hypotenuse. The theorem can be expressed in either algebraic (i.e., linear or sentential) or geometric (i.e., spatial) terms. In like fashion, logical relations can be defined by statements (as in first-order logic

**3** See Valerius Maximus, Memorable Doings and Sayings, vol. II: Books 6–9. Ed. and trans. by David R. Shackleton Bailey (Loeb Classical Library 493). Cambridge MA, London 2000, VIII.7.ext. 7, p. 235: "I should say that Archimedes' diligence also bore fruit if it had not both given him life and taken it away. At the capture of Syracuse Marcellus had been aware that his victory had been held up much and long by Archimedes' machines. However, pleased with the man's exceptional skill, he gave out that his life was to be spared, putting almost as much glory in saving Archimedes as in crushing Syracuse. But as Archimedes was drawing diagrams with mind and eyes fixed on the ground, a soldier who had broken into the house in quest of loot with sword drawn over his head asked him who he was. Too much absorbed in tracking down his objective, Archimedes could not give his name but said, protecting the dust with his hands, 'I beg you, don't disturb this', and was slaughtered as neglectful of the victor's command; with his blood he confused the lines of his art".

**4** For a systematic treatment of the spatial dimensions of diagrams, see Jan Wöpking, Raum und Wissen. Elemente einer Theorie epistemischen Diagrammgebrauchs (Berlin Studies in Knowledge Research 8). Berlin 2016, with references to earlier literature. Wöpking's definition of the diagram, p. 188, in part dependent on Bruno Latour's concept of "immutable mobiles" (see Bruno Latour, Visualisation and Cognition: Drawing Things Together. Knowledge and Society: Studies in the Sociology of Culture Past and Present 6 [1986], pp. 1–40) as "eine externe Inskription" which "(i) auf komplexe, intelligente und wesentliche Weise Raumrelationen nutzt" and "(ii) insofern das Arbeiten mit ihr regelgeleitet, normative ist, (iii) und der Verfolgung epistemischer Zwecke dient", strikes me as too narrow in that it excludes a great deal of diagrammatic material that is neither mathematical nor scientific but still epistemic. One function of diagrams is to lend material that is not necessarily systematic the appearance of normativity. Moreover, as this study seeks to show, while most medieval diagrams externalized and materialized knowledge, they hardly objectified it or succeeded in lending it stability. In applying such criteria, Wöpking, like Latour, overestimates the "optical consistency" of printed images, let alone those found in manuscripts.

**5** The use of color in medieval diagrams awaits comprehensive discussion. In the meantime, see Jeffrey F. Hamburger, Color in Cusanus. Stuttgart 2021.

and Boolean algebra) or by sets (e.g., Euler circles and Venn diagrams). Although cognitive scientists sometimes question whether the two modes of demonstration can be distinguished from one another, they, in like fashion, propose alternating views of mental representation, one based on "Euclidean cognitive maps", the other, on "graph-like representations" (with "graph" understood as it is in graph theory, as a way of representing a network).[6] The diagram presents a way, not simply of representing, but also of thinking about, the world.

**6** See Michael Peer et al., Structuring Knowledge with Cognitive Maps and Cognitive Graphs. Trends in Cognitive Science 25 (2021), pp. 37–54.

# From Plato to Peirce

On the nature of the diagram, Charles Sanders Peirce is precise:

> Hypoicons [instantiations of icons] may be roughly divided according to the mode of Firstness [that is, their pre-reflexive immediacy] of which they partake. Those which partake of simple qualities, or First Firstnesses, are images; those which represent the relations, mainly dyadic, or so regarded, of the parts of one thing by analogous relations in their own parts, are diagrams; those which represent the representative character of a representamen by representing a parallelism in something else, are metaphors.[7]

The diagram is neither a symbol nor an index; rather, it is an icon – but of a particular type. Whereas indices are characterized by a factual correspondence with their object, and symbols by imputed characteristics, icons share qualities with it (as in a red painting of a red rose). Rather than first-order likenesses, diagrams root resemblance in a set of structural relationships shared with that which they represent. These relationships, "mainly dyadic" (as in a one-to-one correspondence), are what render a diagram spatial. In the words of Johanna Drucker, "Diagrammatic images spatialize relations in a meaningful way. They make spatial relations [e.g. simultaneity, hierarchy, juxtaposition, proximity, alignment, connectedness and disconnectedness] meaningful".[8]

A simple line suffices to connect two or more points. Attach identifiers to these points (Peirce's 'analogous relations'), thereby creating a compound object consisting of text and image, and one has a diagram. A diagram of this kind is not as simple as it seems. Plato's Divided Line ('Republic' 509d–511e), philosophy's Ur-diagram, provides an exemplary instance. Speaking to Glaucon, Socrates says:

> 'Imagine a line cut in two. Take two unequal segments and again cut each one in the same ratio, one for the visible class, the other for the intelligible; and you will have in the first segment of the visible section images in relation to each

7 Charles Sanders Peirce, Sundry Logical Conceptions. In: The Essential Peirce. Selected Philosophical Writings, vol. 2. Ed. by the Peirce Edition Project. Bloomington, Indianapolis 1998, pp. 267–288, at p. 274.

8 Johanna Drucker, Graphesis: Visual Forms of Knowledge Production (MetaLABprojects). Cambridge MA 2014, p. 66.

> other by their clarity or obscurity – and by images I mean firstly shadows, the reflections in water and in those surfaces which are solid, smooth and shiny, and everything like this, if you get my meaning'. [Glaucon] 'Well yes, I do'. [Socrates] 'Now take the second section which this one resembles to be the living creatures around us, all natural things and the whole class of artificial things'.[9]

Socrates's first division is between the visible world (the realm of the senses) and the intelligible (the realm of illumination, imagery rooted in the immediately prior passage, the analogy of the sun, according to which the idea of goodness illuminates the intelligible with truth). Each of the two realms is divided in turn, the former between *eikasia* (opinion rooted in empirical cognition or the imagination, often bordering on delusion)[10] and *pistis* (belief rooted in experience), the latter, between *διάνοια* (thought, exemplified by mathematical knowledge) and *noēsis* (intuitive understanding, i.e., dialectic entirely free of likenesses).

For Plato, diagrams, including the Divided Line, whether imagined by the reader or realized in material form, themselves belong to the realm of the senses. Although the diagram assists in leading the mind toward an endpoint (literal as well as argumentative), only the object of the diagram, the idea or set of concepts it represents in terms of the relationship among its parts, can justly claim to consist of knowledge in its pure, intuitive form. In short, the knowledge achieved by the mathematician falls short of that attained by the philosopher.[11]

Plato would disapprove, but the purpose of this essay is to bring diagrams down to earth by underscoring some of the contingencies that affected their production, transmission, and interpretation. Diagrams do not exist in the abstract; they make speculation concrete in ways that inflect their meanings, intentionally or not. Greek mathematicians, who were essentially geometers, may have thought in diagrams so that, in Reviel NETZ's formulation, "the diagram is the metonym of the proposi-

**9** Plato, The Republic. Vol. 1: Books 1–5. Ed. and trans. by Christopher Emlyn-Jones and William Preddy. Cambridge MA 2013, p. 97.

**10** Damien Story, What is *eikasia*? Oxford Studies in Ancient Philosophy 58 (2020), pp. 19–57.

**11** For Plato's use of mathematical diagrams, see Richard Patterson, Diagram, Dialectic, and Mathematical Foundations in Plato. Aperion 40 (2020), pp. 1–34; Duncan F. Kennedy, Metaphysics and the Mathematical Diagram. Geometry between History and Philosophy. In: Pantelis Michelakis (ed.), Classics and Media Theory (Classical Presences). Oxford 2020, pp. 77–114; and Tamsin de Waal, The Mathematicians' Use of Diagrams in Plato. In: Nils Kürbis, Bahram Assadian and Jonathan Nassim (eds.), Knowledge, Number and Reality. Encounters with the Work of Keith Hossack. London 2022, pp. 143–160, with additional bibliography. For Greek mathematicians' use of diagrams outside of philosophy, see Reviel Netz, The Shaping of Deduction in Greek Mathematics. A Study in Cognitive History (Ideas in Context 41). Cambridge 1999.

tion".[12] Plato, however, adopts the diagrammatic language of Greek mathematics for his own metaphysical purposes, a circumstance that constitutes a contingency of its own. Within the hierarchy of cognition charted by the Divided Line, in which intuitive cognition (*noēsis*) surpasses discursive thinking (*dianoia*), the form of *technē* represented by the diagram remains inherently contingent, practical rather than theoretical. This contingency cuts to the heart of what for Plato represents true understanding or wisdom as opposed to technical know-how.[13] Whereas for him, *ἐπιστήμη* (*epistēmē*: knowledge, understanding) stands in opposition to *δόξα* (*doxa*: opinion), in modern discourse, at least following FOUCAULT, the epistemic has come to stand for contingency tout court, in his words, "the conditions of possibility of all knowledge" within a given historical period. Rather than referring to timeless truth, the seeming pleonasm of "epistemic knowledge" refers less to what is known than to the time-bound rules or assumptions by which anything can be known.[14]

The manuscript transmission of diagrams reveals such contingency in very material ways.[15] The earliest extant representation of Plato's Divided Line occurs

**12** Reviel Netz, Greek Mathematical Diagrams. Their Use and Their Meaning. For the Learning of Mathematics 18 (1998), pp. 33–39, at pp. 37–38.

**13** These brief comments hardly do justice to the complexity of the relationship between *episteme* and *techne* in Plato, for which see Richard Parry, *Episteme* and *Techne*. In: The Stanford Encyclopedia of Philosophy (Spring 2024 Edition), available at: https://plato.stanford.edu/archives/spr2024/entries/episteme-techne/ (28/7/2024).

**14** Michel Foucault, The Order of Things. An Archaeology of the Human Sciences. New York 1994, p. 168: "In any given culture, there is always only one *episteme* that defines the conditions of possibility of all knowledge, whether expressed in a theory or silently invested in a practice". – See, e.g., Gary Gutting, Michel Foucault's Archaeology of Scientific Reason (Modern European Philosophy). Cambridge 1989, p. 285: "Foucault proposes, in the end, a twofold transformation of the traditional concept of philosophy. First, he turns it away from the effort at an a priori determination of the essential limits of human thought and action and instead makes it a historical demonstration of the contingency of what present themselves as necessary restrictions. Second, he no longer asks it to provide the justification for the values that guide our lives but instead employs it to clear the path of intellectual obstacles to the achievement of those values".

**15** Although this essay focuses on examples from the Neoplatonic tradition, a similar approach, adumbrated by Michael Krewet, Bilder des Unräumlichen. Zum Erkenntnispotential von Diagrammen in Aristoteleshandschriften. Wiener Studien 127 (2014), pp. 71–100, can also be applied to Aristotelian diagrams. Krewet, p. 86, summarizes Aristotle's position as laid out in 'De Memoria et reminiscentia' I 449b30–450a14 as follows: "Um das Wesen einer Sache, das für sich selbst keine festgelegte Ausdehnung besitzt und nicht an eine bestimmte Materie gebunden ist, erkennen zu können, stellen wir uns das Wesen der Sache vor Augen, indem wir es in seiner Realisierung in einer bestimmten Ausdehnung – und damit bildlich – vorstellen". For diagrams in Aristotelian manuscripts (including commentaries), see Alfred Stückelberg, *Aristotle illustratus*. Anschauungshilfsmittel in der Schule des Peripatos. Museum Helveticum 50 (1992), pp. 131–143.

in a Byzantine manuscript of the late ninth century (Paris, Bibliothèque nationale de France, ms. grec. 1807, fol. 72r), part of a set known as the 'Philosophical Collection' (Fig. 1). [16]

Sybille KRÄMER has suggested that "We cannot dismiss the possibility that the indeterminacy in Plato's descriptions of diagrams is due to the fact that there were practices in place at the Academy which made it clear precisely how Plato's descriptions were to be carried out graphically".[17] Elsewhere, she argues that

**16** As far as I have been able to determine, the sole mention of this diagram in the vast literature that touches on the Divided Line is Sybille Krämer, 'The Mind's Eye'. Visualizing the Non-Visual and the 'Epistemology of the Line'. In: Richard Heinrich et al. (eds.), Image and Imaging in Philosophy, Science and the Arts, vol. 2. Proceedings of the 33rd International Ludwig Wittgenstein Symposium in Kirchberg, 2010, 2011 (Publications of the Austrian Ludwig Wittgenstein Society. New Series 17). Frankfurt et al., pp. 275–293, at pp. 279–281, where, however, its existence is noted but its form and content, let alone the apparent contradictions in its construction, are not discussed. As part of Book VI, it is not included among the diagrammatic scholia to the Republic redrawn in Domenico Cufalo, Scholia Graeca in Platonem. Scholia ad Clitophontem et Reipublicae libros I–V continens. Tesi di Dottorato di Ricerca, Università degli Studi di Pisa 2010–2011, pp. 101–106. It is, however, reproduced schematically in Scholia Platonica. Ed. by William Chase Green. Haverford PA 1938, p. 246 (510d). For the 'Philosophical Collection', see Bernard Flusin, La production byzantine des livres aux siècles VII–VIII. In: Jean-Claude Cheynet (ed.), Le monde byzantin 2: L'Empire byzantin 641–1204. Paris 2006, pp. 346–347; Lidia Perria, Scrittura e ornamentazione nei codici della 'collezione filosofica'. Rivista di studi bizantini e neoellenici 28 (1991), pp. 45–111; Annaclara Palau Cataldi, Un nuovo codice della 'collezione filosofica'. Il palinsesto Parisinus graecus 2575. Scriptorium 55 (2001), pp. 249–274; Filippo Ronconi, La collection brisée. La face cachée de la 'collection philosophique'. Les milieux socioculturels. In: Paolo Oderico (ed.), La face cachée de la littérature byzantine. Le texte en tant que message immédiat. Actes du colloque international, Paris, 5–7 juin 2008. Paris 2012, pp. 137–166; Didier Marcotte, La 'collection philosophique'. Historiographie et histoire des textes. Scriptorium 68 (2014), pp. 145–165; Daniele Bianconi and Filippo Ronconi (eds.), La 'Collection philosophique' face à l'histoire. Péripéties et tradition. Spoleto 2020. For marginal annotations in these manuscripts, see Christian Brockmann, Scribal Annotations as Evidence of Learning in Manuscripts from the First Byzantine Humanism. The 'Philosophical Collection'. In: Jörg B. Quenzer and Dimitri Bondarev (eds.), Manuscript Cultures: Mapping the Field. Berlin, Boston 2014, pp. 11–34.

**17** Sybille Krämer, Is There a Diagrammatic Impulse with Plato? 'Quasi-Diagrammatic Scenes' in Plato's Philosophy. In: Sybille Krämer and Christina Ljungberg (eds.), Thinking with Diagrams. The Semiotic Basis of Human Cognition. Berlin, Boston 2016, pp. 161–177, at pp. 165–166. Among Krämer's many other essays on relevant topics, see ead., Notationen, Schemata, Diagramme. Über 'Räumlichkeit' als Darstellungsprinzip. Sechs kommentierte Thesen. In: Gabriele Brandstetter, Franck Hofmann and Kirsten Maar (eds.), Notationen und choreographisches Denken. Freiburg i. Br. 2010, pp. 27–45; ead., Gedanken sichtbar machen: Platon – Eine diagrammatologische Rekonstruktion. Ein Essay. In: Jan-Henrik Möller, Jörg Sternagel and Lenore Hipper (eds.), Paradoxalität des Medialen. Munich 2013, pp. 175–191; and ead., Point, Line, Surface as Plane. From Notational Iconicity to Diagrammatology. In: Zarco Paic and Kresimir Purgar (eds.), Theorizing Images. Cambridge 2016, pp. 202–227.

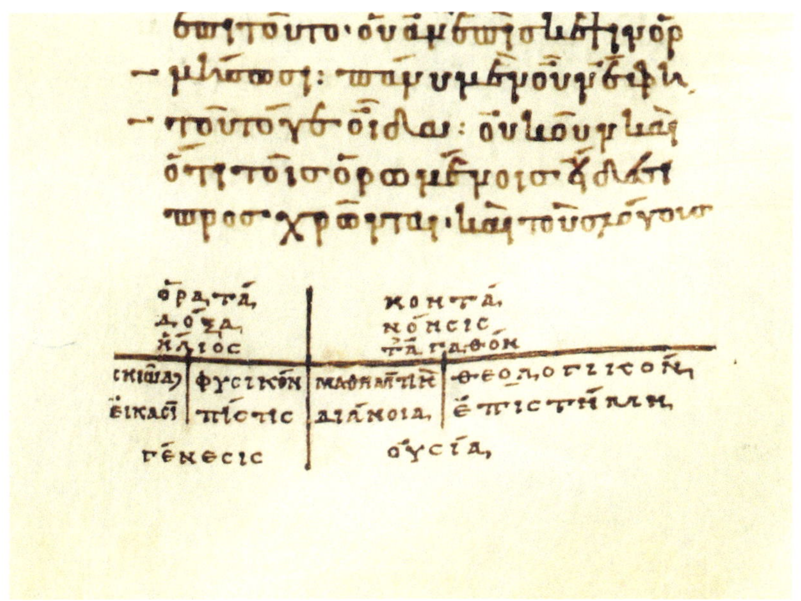

Fig. 1: The Divided Line ('Republic', 509d–511e). Plato, 'Tetralogies', 8–9, Constantinople, 850–875. Paris, Bibliothèque nationale de France, ms. gr. 1807, fol. 72r (detail). Photo: BnF.

"although the procedure of diairesis is transmitted to us in the Platonic dialogues only in written form, we can proceed from the assumption that it corresponded to actual visualizations".[18] But can we?

**18** Sybille Krämer, Figuration, Anschauung, Erkenntnis. Grundlinien einer Diagrammatologie (Suhrkamp Taschenbuch Wissenschaft 2176). Berlin 2016, p. 171: "Obwohl also das Verfahren der Dihairesis uns in den platonischen Dialogen nur in Textform überliefert ist, können wir davon ausgehen, dass ihm reale Visualisierungen entsprachen". My translation.

# The Scene of the Diagram

Almost 1500 years separate the earliest extant manuscripts of Plato's works (the Clarke Plato, Oxford, Bodleian Library, MS. Clarke 39, and the manuscript in Paris) from their author. This period witnessed profound changes, not only in the reception of classical texts, but also in the way in which they were written (in a new minuscule script), annotated (often with an extensive marginal apparatus), and disseminated.[19] Even had Byzantine scholars of the ninth and tenth centuries possessed an ancient Greek copy of Plato (which they did not), they would have understood its diagrammatic illustrations, assuming there were any, in their own distinctive way.

This farfetched hypothetical poses the question of whether diagrams must always take the form of external representations. In some cases, mostly mathematical, almost certainly yes, but in others, primarily philosophical (such as Meno's thought experiment with the slave boy in Plato's dialogue of the same name), most likely not. Reading diagrams requires a set of skills, which developed and changed over time. Just as the shift from the oral to the written transmission of works transformed what it meant to speak of a "text" (making them more stable objects, if not as fixed as we are accustomed to thinking of them today), so too, the transition from an oral to a written setting altered the understanding and application of diagrams.[20] The mental manipulation of a diagram need not have always required their external realization. Even had it done so, diagrams drawn

**19** Brockmann (note 16), pp. 11–34. See also Pasquale Orsini, Pratiche collettive di scrittura a Bisanzio nei secoli IX e X. Segno e Testo: International Journal of Manuscripts and Text Transmission 3 (2005), pp. 265–342.

**20** On this point, see Netz (note 12), p. 39: "they [the Greeks] did not develop mathematical notation. Because of this, they relied much more heavily upon oral aids, such as oral formulae. The verbal was typically used in the oral mode. In mathematics, then, on the one hand, the Greeks did not develop anything like our modern written symbols; on the other, they did develop a system of formulaic expressions, one which is essentially oral. They were therefore in a sense oral both in what they did not do and in what they did do. I am convinced that much of their mathematical reasoning took the shape of a silent soliloquy, unaided by writing, in front of a diagram". For the fixity of medieval texts (or lack thereof), see Marilynn Desmond, The Visuality of Reading in Pre-Modern Textual Cultures. Australian Journal of French Studies 46 (2009), pp. 219–234, one of many such studies that could be cited.

extemporaneously in the dust would have functioned differently than the textbook diagrams with which we are familiar today. In the words of Reviel NETZ, referring to ancient Greek mathematical diagrams, they served a performative function: "one took the concrete, schematic diagram, and invested it, in one's imagination, with the full information it was required to carry". He continues:

> The fundamental point [was] that reading, in general, was expected to involve such work of interpretation. The precise position of ancient writing – schematic, and yet pointing at something made vivid to the mind – made it very natural to embed, within it, this special object, so significant to Greek mathematics: the schematic diagram, made-believe to be the geometrical thing itself.[21]

Although writing centuries later than the Hellenistic period addressed by NETZ, Augustine, in his 'Confessions' IV.16, speaks to a similar *mise-en-scène* in ways that reveal significant continuities and discontinuities:

> What good did it do me that at about the age of twenty there came into my hands a work of Aristotle which they call the 'Ten Categories'? My teacher in rhetoric at Carthage, and others too who were reputed to be learned men, used to speak of this work with their cheeks puffed out with conceit, and at the very name I gasped with suspense as if about to read something great and divine. Yet I read it without any expositor and understood it. I had discussions with people who said that they had understood the 'Categories' only with much difficulty after the most erudite teachers had not only given oral explanation but had drawn numerous diagrams in the dust [*sed multa in pulvere depingentibus*]. They could tell me nothing they had learnt from these teachers which I did not already know from reading the book on my own without having anyone explain it.[22]

As noted by James O'DONNELL in reference to this passage, "[w]hat Augustine reads as a sign of intuition on his part is at the same time a fragment of the history of literacy. Where other students could approach the text only through the medium of oral discussion [of which, it should be noted, the recourse to diagrams drawn in the dust constituted a critical part], Augustine has mastered the skills

**21** Reviel Netz, Why Were Greek Mathematical Diagrams Schematic? Nuncius 35 (2020), pp. 506–535, at p. 535.
**22** St. Augustine, Confessions. Trans. by Henry Chadwick. Oxford 2008, p. 69.

of purely textual manipulation".[23] Augustine situates himself in a context in which diagrams move from the ground on which a given group was gathered to the plane of the page.[24] Solitary, perhaps even silent, reading already existed in antiquity, but Augustine testifies to a shift in the scene of instruction: from an oral setting, in which participants in a dialogue share ideas in a quasi-public forum to that of private reading and study. From his account, however, which stresses that others required the aid of diagrams yet implies that he did not, it cannot be inferred that the text from which he taught himself without the aid of oral instruction contained the diagrams to which he refers.

Over time, however, the spaces of knowledge shift, as do its objects.[25] By the time of the rhetorician C. Marius Victorinus (c. 300–after 362) and the polymath Cassiodorus (c. 485–c. 585), diagrams already had an established place in the codex.[26] They had become external aids to cognition. In their landmark essay on the theory of the extended mind, Andy CLARK and David CHALMERS argue that, "[i]f, as we confront some task, a part of the world functions as a process which, *were it done in the head*, we would have no hesitation in recognizing as part of the

**23** James J. O'Donnell, Augustine. 'Confessions', 3 vols. Oxford 1992, vol. 2, p. 265.

**24** The transition in question is by no means completed with Augustine; see John D. Schaeffer, The Dialectic of Orality and Literacy. The Case of Book 4 of Augustine's 'De Doctrina Christiana'. In: Richard Leo Enos et al. (eds.), The Rhetoric of Saint Augustine of Hippo: 'De doctrina Christiana' and the Search for a Distinctly Christian Rhetoric (Studies in Rhetoric and Religion 7). Waco TX 2008, pp. 289–310, at p. 307: "The 'De doctrina' presents concepts of reading, praying, and style that are informed by Augustine's attempt to bring classical rhetoric, a discipline associated with extemporaneous oral performance, to bear on Christian preaching, which was grounded in the interpretation of a written text. The profound and glacial changes that occurred while European culture was adopting Christianity, a textually based religion, are documented, at least partially, in book 4 of the 'De doctrina', where Augustine attempts to transform rhetoric into a tool for oral expression of interior states formed by reading and prayer. But even reading and prayer are still orally controlled in book 4, for Augustine has not interiorized silent reading or private meditation to the extent that modern Western subjects have".

**25** Cf. Netz (note 12), p. 39: "but the one fixed, solid object in Greek mathematics was not the word, but the picture. This was actually drawn, not just spoken, and therefore it was actually out there, it was the physical reality, the inter-subjective definite object. [...] The verbal could not be the fixed object in Greek mathematics because of the more oral approach taken in Greek mathematics".

**26** For Victorinus, see Thomas Riesenweber, C. Marius Victorinus. 'Commenta in Ciceronis Rhetorica', 2 vols. Boston, Berlin 2015; for Cassiodorus, Michael Gorman, The Diagrams in the Oldest Manuscripts of Cassiodorus' 'Institutiones'. Revue Bénédictine 110 (2000), pp. 27–41, at p. 30: "Diagrams were an integral part of the 'Institutiones' as planned and executed by Cassiodorus".

cognitive process, then that part of the world *is* […] part of the cognitive process."[27] Diagrams, albeit manmade, are just such a 'part of the world'. Yet what constitutes a diagram very much depends on how such an object – an object of thought or an actual object – works in a particular context. In effect, the diagrams invoked in Plato's dialogues demand an inversion of CLARK and CHALMERS's hypothetical: if, as we confront some task for which we now rely on an external aid (such as a diagram or, for that matter, a computer), we cannot conclude that for people living the better part of two and a half millennia before our time, that same task could not in some cases have been done in the head. Most of us also cannot recite poems the length of the 'Iliad' and the 'Odyssey' by heart.

**27** Andy Clark and David J. Chalmers, The Extended Mind. Analysis 58 (1998), pp. 7–19, at p. 8. For further discussion (and demurral), see Richard Menary (ed.), The Extended Mind. Cambridge MA 2010.

# The Divided Line

In short, even if the diagram of the Divided Line in the manuscript in Paris provided a mirror image of Plato's diagram, it would still not be his insofar as the context of its generation and reception had changed in fundamental ways over the millennium that separates the philosopher from Augustine. Moreover, the diagram depicts not only the line but also additional tiers elaborating, as does Plato, its epistemological and metaphysical meanings.[28] The diagram reads as follows:

<table>
<tr><td colspan="2">ὁρατά (visible [things])<br>δόξα (belief)<br>ἥλιος (sun)</td><td colspan="2">νοητά (intelligible [things])<br>νόησις (intuitive cognition)<br>τ᾽ ἀγαθόν (the good)</td></tr>
<tr><td>σκιῶδ(ες) (shadowy)<br>εἰκασία (conjecture)</td><td>φυσικόν (physical)<br>πίστις (belief)</td><td>μαθημ(α)τικ(όν) (mathematical)<br>διάνοια (discursive reason)</td><td>θεολογικόν (theological)<br>ἐπιστήμη (knowledge / science)</td></tr>
<tr><td colspan="2">γένεσις (becoming)</td><td colspan="2">οὐσία (being)</td></tr>
</table>

Short verticals protruding from the horizontal of the divided line itself transform the line into a plane equivalent to that of the parchment page and lend the diagram the appearance of a table, thereby enabling a more complex set of correlations. The line provides the backbone, but the verticals, the ribs. In this version of the diagram, lines and the spaces they define signify equally.

Modern reconstructions of Plato's Divided Line imagine it as just that, a single line ($\alpha\beta$) partitioned, in keeping with Socrates's instructions to Glaucon ('Republic' 509d6–8), at $\gamma$ into two unequal segments of which the first, longer segment ($\alpha\gamma$) stands for the invisible realm, the second, shorter segment ($\gamma\beta$), for the visible. Socrates in turn instructs his interlocutor to divide each of these segments by the ratio governing the initial division. What results is a fourfold division, in which the two intermediary segments ($\delta\gamma$ and $\gamma\varepsilon$) are equal in length. As denoted in

**28** The manuscript later belonged to Florentine, the daughter of Lorenzo di Piero de' Medici, Duke of Urbino, and queen of Henry II of France. For a description and bibliography, see the Pinakes database, diktyon 51433: https://pinakes.irht.cnrs.fr/notices/cote/51433/ (16/1/2024). The manuscript also includes a genealogy of Plato (fol. 115v), a diagram that recurs in somewhat different form in Paris, Bibliothèque nationale de France, ms. Coislin 322, fol. 49v, a copy of Proclus's commentary on the 'Timaeus', for which see Pinakes, diktyon 49463: https://pinakes.irht.cnrs.fr/notices/cote/49463/ (16/1/2024).

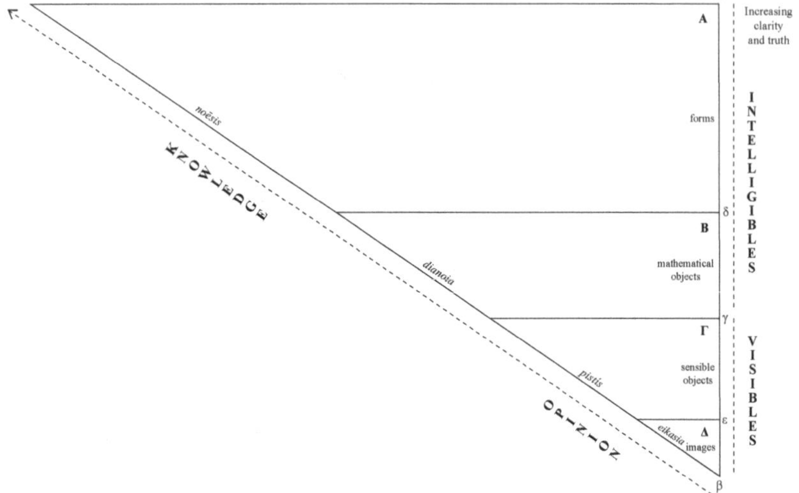


Fig. 2: The Divided Line, with Most of the Constructions Removed but Implicit, as Reconstructed by Terry ECHTERLING. Photo: ECHTERLING, What Did Glaucon Draw?, p. 11.

the Byzantine rendition of the diagram, the two parts of the section standing for the visible (the realm of becoming) stand, respectively, for the realms of shadowy conjecture and of physical evidence; the two parts of the section standing for the invisible (the realm of being), for discursive reason, represented by mathematics, and, ultimately, for what Plato calls dialectic, but which in the Byzantine rendition, tellingly, is called theology (*θεολογικόν*).

As Terry ECHTERLING observes and as others have noted, envisaging the Divided Line solely in linear terms introduces "an apparent contradiction between the initial instructions for dividing the line ('Republic' 509d6–8) and the later description of the line's divisions ('Republic' 511e2–4)." "If", he notes, "the two middle segments of the divided line are, and must be, equal, in conformity with Socrates's explicit instructions, then the illustration fails to exhibit the greater degree of clarity and truth as one moves up the line".[29] Translating Plato's process for dividing the line

**29** Terry Echterling, What Did Glaucon Draw? A Diagrammatic Proof for Plato's Divided Line. Journal of the History of Philosophy 56 (2018), pp. 1–15, at p. 3, with reference to previous hypotheses and debates.

into geometric, i.e., two-dimensional rather than one-dimensional, terms, however – a process that in keeping with the procedures of Greek geometry as practiced in Plato's day would have depended on the use of a compass and straightedge (not a ruler) – allows one to conclude that Plato's "diagram could not have been linear, and that, in keeping with Plato's insistence that images are unreliable, must have enabled the observer to distinguish what is central from what is peripheral".[30] The resulting construction generates not a line but rather a two-dimensional diagram in which the segments standing for the different levels of cognition are represented by areas proportional to their place in the hierarchy (Fig. 2).

In short, the Divided Line as presented by Plato only makes sense when viewed in spatial as opposed to linear terms.

**30** Ibid., p. 7. For the unreliability of images in relation to the Divided Line, see Yancy Hughes Dominick, Seeing Through Images. The Bottom of Plato's Divided Line. Journal of the History of Philosophy 48 (2010), pp. 1–13.

# Dimensions of Diairesis in the Pseudo-Dionysius

What is the relationship of line and plane in medieval diagrams, and how does it change over time? Perverse thought it might seem, in seeking to address this question, I sideline Euclidean diagrams, in which, in keeping with Plato's understanding, points, lines, and planes are nothing more than representations of the same, even if they can generate surplus meanings.[31] In the words of a dyed-in-the-wool Platonist, Nicholas of Cusa,

> if we are speaking of visible shape or roundness, which is in no respect true or perfect roundness. For roundness that could not be more round is not at all visible. For since the surface of a [true] sphere is everywhere equally distant from its center, the outer-extremity of what is [perfectly] round – given that it ends at an indivisible point – remains altogether invisible to our eyes. For we see only what is divisible and quantitative.[32]

Like Cusa, who thought of mathematics as an integral, indeed, foundational, part of sound theological inquiry, I am concerned with the basic geometry of diagrams but, no less, their symbolic dimensions.[33] At issue here is how diagrams were perceived and employed historically, not the question, much debated since the nineteenth century, whether they can serve as vehicles of valid reasoning, which has less to do with whether diagrams can aid in conceiving or understanding a mathematical

**31** For diagrams in Euclidean geometry during the Middle Ages, see Wöpking (note 4).
**32** Nicholas of Cusa, De ludo globi (The Bowling Game). Trans. by Jasper Hopkins. Minneapolis MN 2000, I.8, p. 1185. From the large literature on the treatise, I cite only David Albertson, Mapping the Space of God. Mystical 'Weltbilder' in Nicholas of Cusa and the Structure of 'De ludo globi' (1463). In: Philipp Billion (ed.), Weltbilder im Mittelalter = Perceptions of the World in the Middle Ages. Bonn 2009, pp. 61–81; and Marc Föcking, *Serio ludere*. Epistemologie, Spiel und Dialog in Nicolaus Cusanus' 'De ludo globi'. In: Klaus W. Hempfer and Helmut Pfeiffer (eds.), Spielwelten. Performanz und Inszenierung in der Renaissance (Text und Kontext 16). Stuttgart 2022, pp. 1–18.
**33** For the place of geometry in Nicholas of Cusa's philosophy, see David Albertson, Mathematical Theologies. Nicholas of Cusa and the Legacy of Thierry of Chartres (Oxford Studies in Historical Theology). Oxford 2014.

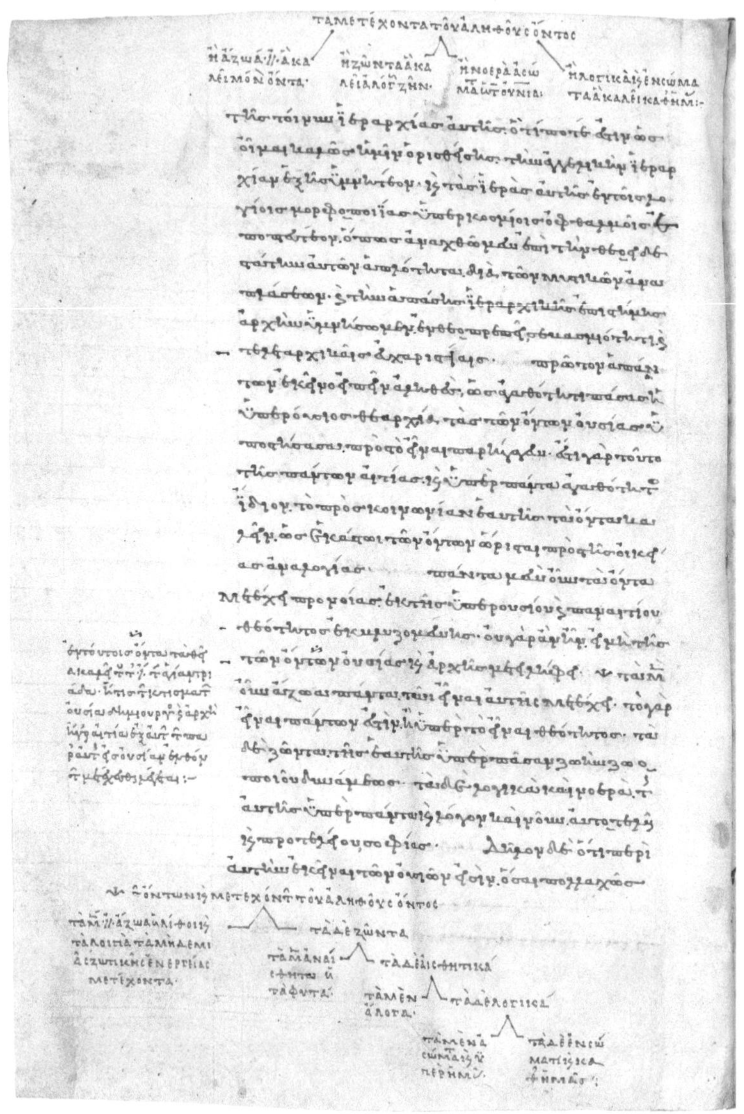

Fig. 3: "Things participating in True Being" and "Of Things that exist and participate in True Being" ('Celestial Hierarchy' 4.1–2; Greek Diagrams 10–11). Ps.-Dionysius, 'Opera', Constantinople, mid-ninth century. Biblioteca Apostolica Vaticana, Vat. gr. 2249, fol. 70v (detail). Photo: BAV.

construction than whether one can trust inferences reached by working from a geometrical figure.[34]

Take, for example, a branching diagram, otherwise known as a diairesis diagram, used in logic to reach definitions through division. The diagram comes from a manuscript of the writings of Dionysius that is roughly contemporary with that from which the previously discussed diagram of the Divided Line was taken (Biblioteca Apostolica Vaticana, Vat. gr. 2249, fol. 70v) (Fig. 3).

It too formed part of the 'Philosophical Collection' and is one of the earliest manuscripts of the Dionysian corpus in which the diagrams that remained a standard part of its scholia until the end of the Middle Ages appear. Rooted in diagrammatic techniques inherited from the Platonic scholia, which in turn reflect the central place of diairesis as a technique in some of Plato's dialogues, the diagrams appear to have been invented by Maximus the Confessor as part of the scholia that he added to the apparatus which accrued from an early date around the corpus.[35]

The diagram (in fact, a pair of diagrams, one in the upper, the other in the lower margin of the manuscript Vat. gr. 2249, fol. 70[v]) accompanies and clarifies the following passage in the 'Celestial Hierarchy' 4.1–2:

> The holy ranks, then, of the heavenly beings, share in the participation of the divine gifts in a higher degree than things which merely exist, or which lead an irrational life, or which are rational like ourselves. For by moulding themselves intellectually to the divine imitation, and looking from the earthly to the divine likeness, and striving to mould their own spiritual likeness after its example, they

**34** See Sun-Joo Shin, Oliver Lemon and John Mumma, Diagrams. In: The Stanford Encyclopedia of Philosophy (Winter 2018 Edition), available at: https://plato.stanford.edu/archives/win2018/entries/diagrams/ (28/7/2024); and Mikkel Willum Johansen, What's in a Diagram? On the Classification of Symbols, Figures and Diagrams. In: Lorenzo Magnani (ed.), Model-Based Reasoning in Science and Technology. Theoretical and Cognitive Issues. Berlin, Heidelberg 2014, pp. 89–108, both with extensive bibliographies.

**35** For the attribution of the diagrams to Maximus, see my forthcoming book, Jeffrey F. Hamburger, The Areopagite through the Ages. For the now standard account of the development of the textual glosses, see Beate Regina Suchla, Dionysius Areopagita. Leben – Werk – Wirkung. Freiburg i. Br. 2008; and for skepticism Caroline Macé, Living Bodies of Texts. The 'Corpus Nazianzenum' and the 'Corpus Dionysiacum'. In: Caroline Macé with Michael Muthreich (eds.), Organizing a Literary Corpus in the Middle Ages (Instrumenta Patristica et Mediaevalia 96). Turnhout 2024, pp. 7–39.

naturally have more ungrudging communications with it, being near and ever moving upwards, as far as permissible.[36]

Corresponding to this passage, which itself employs spatial metaphors, the upper diagram reads as follows:

*τὰ μετέχοντα τοῦ ἀληθοῦς ὄντος* ("Things participating in True Being")
*Ἢ ἄζωα εἰσὶν ἃ καλεῖ μόνον ὄντα* ("Either they are without life, which he calls 'things that merely exist'")
*Ἢ ζῶντα ἃ λέγει ἀλόγως ζῆν* ("Or living, which he says live irrationally")
*Ἢ νοερὰ ἀσώματα ὡς τὰ οὐρανία* ("Or intelligent incorporeal, like celestial things")
*Ἢ λογικὰ (καὶ) ἐνσώματα ἃ καλεῖ καθ' ἡμ(ᾶς)* ("Or rational and corporeal, which he calls 'like ourselves'")

In keeping with the rules of diairesis, these four categories are broken down further by the diagram in the lower margin:

*τῶν ὄντων καὶ μετεχόντων τοῦ ἀληθοῦς ὄντος* ("Of things that exist and participate in True Being")
*Τὰ μὲν (ἐισιν) ἄζωα (ὡς) λίθοι καὶ λοιπὰ τὰ μηδεμιᾶς ζωτικῆς ἐνεργείας μετέχοντα* ("Some are without life like rocks and other things that participate in no vital energy")
*τὰ δὲ ζῶντα* ("Others [are] living")
*τὰ μὲν ἀναίσθητα (ὡς) φυτά* ("Some without perception, like plants")
*τὰ δὲ αἰσθητικά* ("Others perceptive")
*τὰ μὲν ἄλογα* ("Some irrational")
*τὰ δὲ λογικά* ("Others rational")
*τὰ μὲν ἀσώματα ὑπὲρ ἡμᾶς* ("Some, incorporeal [and] superior to us")
*τὰ δὲ ἐνσώματα καὶ καθ` ἡμᾶς* ("Others, corporeal and like us")

Whereas the upper diagram takes the form of a fourfold division in which all the categories of being occupy the same level, in its elaboration, the division proceeds

**36** Corpus Dionysiacum. Ed. by Beate Regina Suchla et al., 4 vols. (Patristische Texte und Studien 33, 36, 62, 79). Berlin, Boston 1990, 1991, 2011, 2021, vol. 2, p. 21.1–7; Pseudo-Dionysius, The Celestial and Ecclesiastical Hierarchy of Dionysius the Areopagite. Trans. by John Parker. London 1894, pp. 23–24.

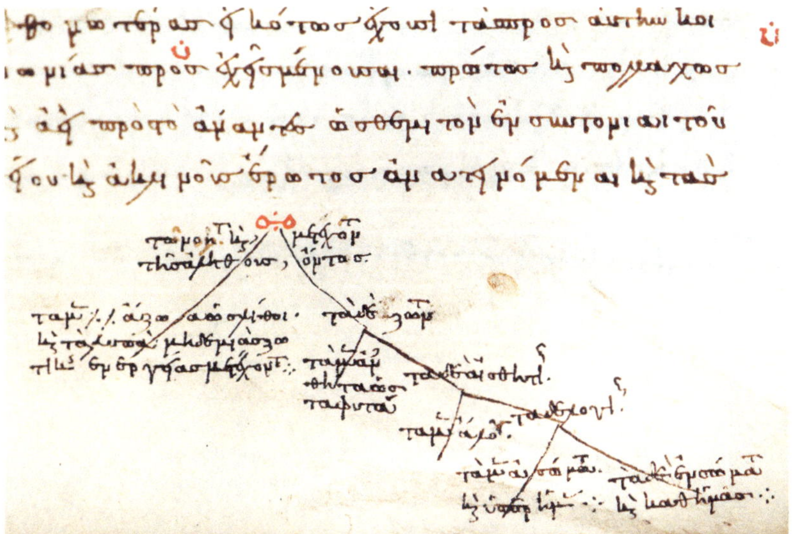

Fig. 4: "Of Things that exist and participate in True Being" ('Celestial Hierarchy' 4.1–2; Greek Diagram 11). Ps.-Dionysius, 'Opera', origin unknown, ninth century. Rome, Biblioteca Vallicelliana, ms. E. 29, fol. 77r (detail). Photo: Biblioteca Vallicelliana.

stepwise from left to right, with the second term of each division being divided again, a directionality that assumes significance in terms of both priority and progression.[37]

The sloping, rightward directionality of the diagram, however, is not de rigeur: in another ninth-century manuscript (Rome, Biblioteca Vallicelliana, ms. E. 29, fol. 77r), the discreet parts of the descending division have been connected into one continuous diagonal (Fig. 4).

**37** Krämer (note 18), p. 173: "Das Definieren ist der Weg durch das Feld der zweigeteilten Begriffe, der (i) von oben nach unten verläuft und (ii) stets die rechte – und nicht etwa die linke – Abzweigung zu nehmen hat". See also ead., Kartographischer Impuls und operative Bildlichkeit. Eine Reflexion über Karten und die Bedeutung räumlicher Orientierung beim Erkennen. Zeitschrift für Kulturwissenschaften 1 (2018), pp. 19–32.

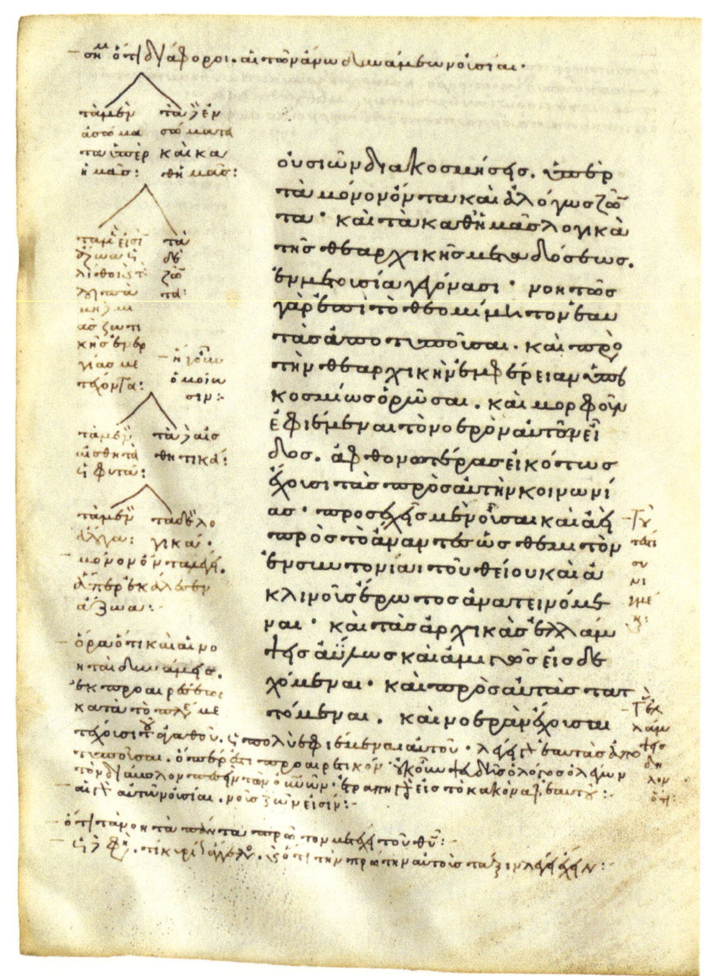

Fig. 5: "Of Things that exist and participate in True Being" ('Celestial Hierarchy' 4.1–2; Greek Diagram 11). Ps.-Dionysius, 'Opera', origin unknown, twelfth century. Paris, Bibliothèque nationale de France, ms. Coislin 86, fol. 193v. Photo: BnF.

In a copy of the fifteenth or sixteenth century (London, British Library, Add. MS. 82952, fol. 15r), the first three steps descend before, perhaps for lack of space, the fourth rises.

In a thirteenth-century copy (British Library, Add. MS. 22350, fol. 22v), the progression splits in two for the same reason. A codex of the twelfth century (Paris, Bibliothèque nationale de France, ms. Coislin 86, fol. 193v), stacks up the four stages of the diairesis in the outer margin due to lack of space to unfold them laterally (Fig. 5).

Given such constraints, the clarity of the arrangement could quickly degenerate. In some manuscripts (e.g., Oxford, Magdalen College, gr. 2, fol. 17r; Bibliothèque nationale de France, ms. gr. 444, fol. 13v; Sinai, Cod. 319, fol. 20v; Sinai, Cod. 322, fol. 14v), the descending ladder of terms takes the form of a flourish that, not unlike a hasty signature, devolves into a trailing zigzag line after three linked dichotomies (Fig. 6).

In this case, it appears that one scribe's hastiness was treated too reverently as a canonical form. The most dramatic transformation, however, occurs in an eleventh-century copy (Rome, Biblioteca Vallicelliana, ms. B. 55, fol. 25r) in which the diairesis filling the lower margin assumes a form resembling nothing so much as a mountainous landscape (Fig. 7).

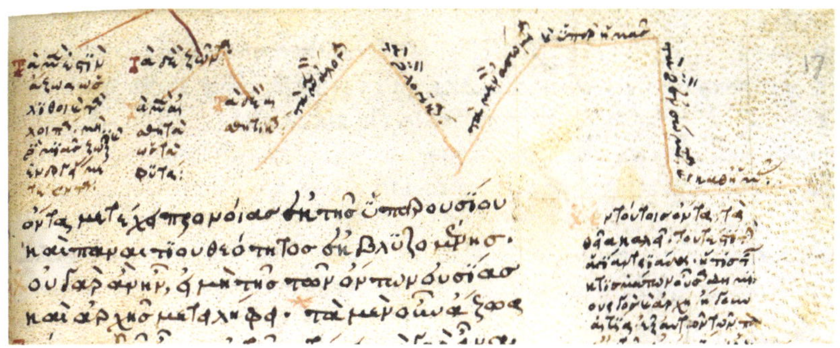

Fig. 6: "Of Things that exist and participate in True Being" ('Celestial Hierarchy' 4.1–2; Greek Diagram 11). Ps.-Dionysius, 'Opera', Constantinople, 1325–1350. Oxford, Magdalen College Library, gr. 2, fol. 17r (detail). Photo: The President and Fellows of Magdalen College, Oxford.

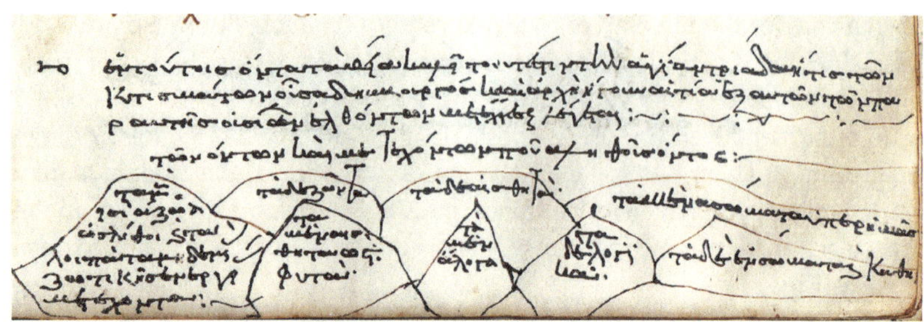

Fig. 7: "Of Things that exist and participate in True Being" ('Celestial Hierarchy' 4.1–2; Greek Diagram 11). Ps.-Dionysius, 'Opera', origin unknown, eleventh century. Rome, Biblioteca Vallicelliana, ms. B. 55, fol. 25r (detail). Photo: Biblioteca Vallicelliana.

If spatial disposition acquires meaning in these manuscripts, then it is in highly divergent and often contingent ways. Greek mathematical diagrams present similar problems; as observed by Ken SAITO and Nathan SIDOLI, they are

> historically contingent objects which were read and copied and redrawn many times over the centuries. In some cases, they may tell us about ancient practice, in other cases, about medieval interpretations of ancient practice, and in some few cases, they simply tell us about the idiosyncratic reading of a single scribe.[38]

At issue is less the diagram's codicological disposition or the scribe's skill (or sloppiness) but rather the diagram's function within a specific communicative setting.[39] In the words of James ELKINS, contrary to the notion that "schemata, diagrams, graphs, and tables are among the images that are [...] overwhelmingly, obdurately inexpressive and geared towards the cold transmission of information", diagrams enjoy "'degrees of freedom'" that enable them to convey "personal, political, social, psychological, gendered or other kinds of meaning that artists can more or less freely incorporate into their works. [...] They can be discussed using the language

**38** Ken Saito and Nathan Sidoli, Diagrams and Arguments in Ancient Greek Mathematics. Lessons Drawn from Comparisons of the Manuscript Diagrams with Those in Modern Critical Editions. In: Karine Chemla (ed.), The History of Mathematical Proof in Ancient Traditions. Cambridge 2012, pp. 135–160, at p. 140.

**39** Ibid., p. 157: "The indifference to visual accuracy implies that the diagram was not meant to be a visual depiction of the objects under discussion but rather to use visual cues to communicate the important mathematical relationships. In this sense, the diagrams are schematic representations".

of Western fine-art images and assigned expressive as well as informational meaning".[40] The Dionysian diagrams provide ample proof of this proposition.

In the diagrams to the Dionysian corpus, epistemology and ontology are welded into one. Levels of knowing correspond to levels of being. Philosophy acquires a topography. Whether implicitly or explicitly, diagrams chart this space of knowledge. The grafting of levels of being onto levels of knowing constitutes one of the central themes in Dionysius's thought. Indeed, 'hierarchy' is a word that Dionysius is credited with having invented (although he probably adopted it from Proclus). He defines it in the 'Celestial Hierarchy' 3.1:

> Hierarchy is, in my judgment, a sacred order and science and energy – assimilated, as far as is permissible, to the likeness of God, and conducted to the illuminations granted to itself from God, in due order, with a view to divine imitation. Now the divine attractiveness, as being uncompounded, as good, as source of initiation, is altogether free from any dissimilarity. But it imparts its own proper light to each according to their fitness, and perfects in most divine initiation in proportion to the unvarying likeness of those who are being initiated into harmony with itself. [...] For each of those who have been called into the hierarchy find their perfection in being caried to the divine initiation in their own proper degree; and, what is more divine than all, as the oracles say, in becoming a fellow-worker with God, and in shewing the divine energy dwelling in itself, manifested as far as possible to others. For it is an hierarchical regulation that some are purified and that others purify; that some are enlightened and others enlighten; that some are perfected and others perfect. So that each one will accomplish the divine imitation in his own several manners.[41]

In light of its complexity, it comes as no surprise that the scholia to Dionysius sought to clarify this passage with a three-part diaresis diagram that lends spatial embodiment to the underlying ideas. One finds this three-part diagram – which supplies a synthesis in that the term Ἡ θεία μακαριότης (Divine Beatitude) is not introduced until section 3.2 – in perhaps its purest form in the same ninth-century manuscript to which I have turned previously (Vat. gr. 2249, fol. 69v) (Fig. 8):

**40** James Elkins, The Domain of Images. Ithaca NY 1999, p. 13.
**41** Corpus Dionysiacum (note 36), vol. 2, pp. 17.3–9; 18.14–19.3; The Celestial and Ecclesiastical Hierarchy (note 36), pp. 21–22.

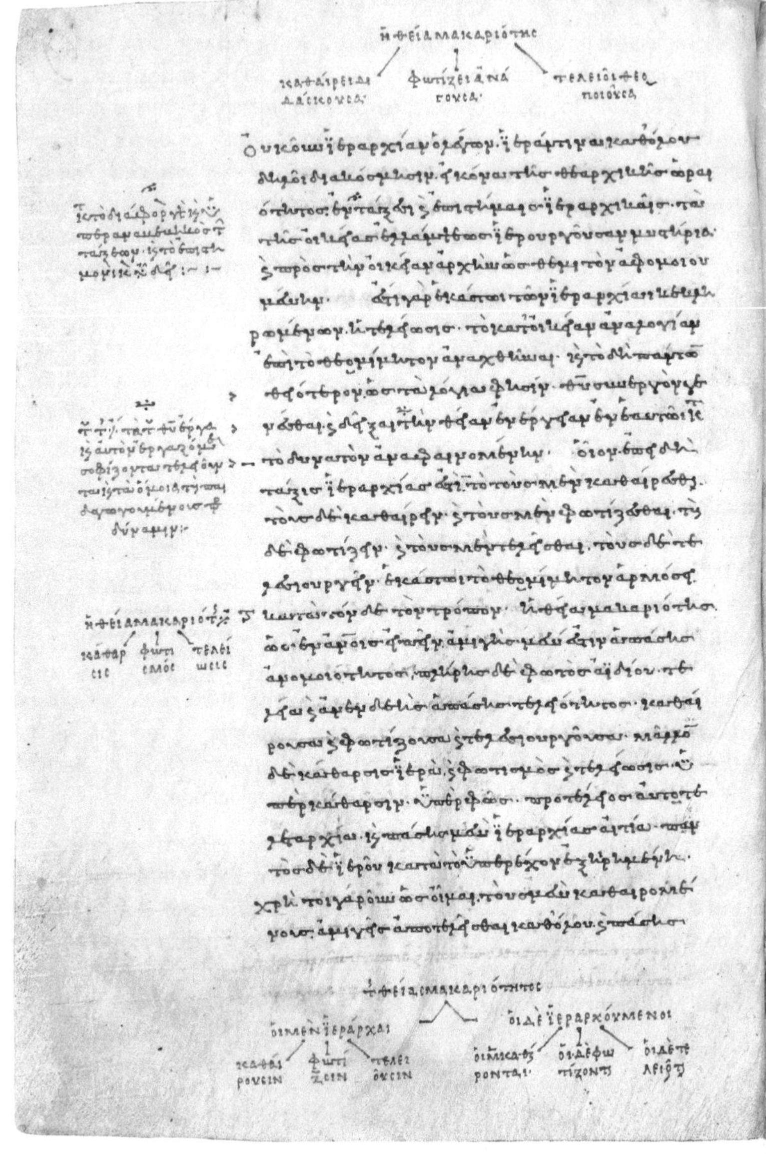

Fig. 8: "Divine Beatitude" and "Purification, Illumination, and Perfection" ('Celestial Hierarchy' 3.1–2; Greek Diagram 9). Ps.-Dionysius, 'Opera', Constantinople, mid-ninth century. Biblioteca Apostolica Vaticana, Vat. gr. 2249, fol. 69v. Photo: BAV.

i) Ἡ θεία μακαριότης ("Divine Beatitude")
καθαίρει διδάσκουσα ("Purifies by teaching")
φωτίζει ἀνάγουσα ("Illuminates by enlightening")
τελειοῖ θεοποιοῦσα ("Perfects by deifying")

ii) Ἡ θεία μακαριότης ("Divine Beatitude")
κάθαρσις ("Purification")
φωτισμός ("Illumination")
τελείωσις ("Perfection")

iii) Τῆς θείας μακαριότητος ("Of the Divine Beatitude")
Οἱ μὲν ἱεράρχαι ("Hierarchs, on the one hand")
καθαίρουσι ("Purify")
φωτίζουσι ("Illuminate")
τελειοῦσι ("Perfect")
Οἱ δὲ ἱεαρχούμενοι ("Those being initiated into the hierarchy")
οἱ μὲν καθαίρονται ("Some are purified")
οἱ δὲ φωτίζονται ("Others are enlightened")
οἱ δὲ τελειοῦνται ("Others are perfected")

In keeping with the dynamic, reciprocal character of Dionysian hierarchy, the diagram stresses the upward *reditus* as much as the downward *exitus*. Those who purify, illuminate, and perfect are matched by those who are purified, illuminated, and directed, so that the whole of creation becomes akin to a house of mirrors in which the goal is to reflect the source of the image as perfectly as possible. The diagrams articulate how divine beatitude circulates through the Dionysian system defined by outflowing and inflowing from and to the Godhead.

Within this hierarchy, each level remains discrete, imparting "its own proper light to each according to their fitness, and perfecting in most divine initiation in proportion to the unvarying likeness of those who are being initiated into harmony with itself".[42] At the same time, however, the hierarchy's ultimate purpose is to lead all things back into the unity from which it initially unfolded: "The scope, then, of hierarchy is the assimilation and oneness with God" ('Celestial Hierarchy' 3.1) of each being in so far as it is possible.[43] Hierarchy is less a separation of levels than it

**42** Corpus Dionysiacum (note 36), vol. 2, p. 17.7–9; The Celestial and Ecclesiastical Hierarchy (note 36), p. 21.
**43** Corpus Dionysiacum (note 36), vol. 2, p. 17.10–11; The Celestial and Ecclesiastical Hierarchy (note 36), p. 21.

is a scaffolding by which one can ascend from one level to the next. The hierarchy is not static, like the rungs on a ladder – an image often enlightening in such contexts; rather, with reference to the entities which participate in it, it is dynamic, so that a more apropos metaphor might be paired descending and ascending escalators or, to use the medieval equivalent, the angels descending and ascending Jacob's ladder.[44]

Rather than simply echoing the text, the diagrams comment on it. They supplement the text by linking each of the three 'ways' with an additional activity, in succession teaching, uplifting, and deifying. In so doing, it anticipates the closing section of the chapter ('Celestial Hierarchy' 3.3), in which, as it were, Dionysius speaks to the qualifications required for participation at each of the three levels. The diagram demonstrates that its purpose, far from a simple outline of the text, is to provide a digest or synthesis.

How this hierarchy is visualized, however, very much depends on codicological considerations. It might have made more sense to place the second diagram, which simply lays out the three ways, purification, illumination, and perfection, in ascending order, at the beginning of the sequence, to be followed by the first, which turns from the activities or processes themselves to the manner in which those processes are enacted, through teaching, uplifting, and deifying, after which the third clarifies who does the teaching, enlightening, and deifying (the hierarchs), and who is taught, uplifted, and deified (those being initiated into the hierarchy). Some scribes clearly had similar thoughts. In some manuscripts (e.g., Add. MS. 22350, fol. 20v, of the thirteenth century), the sequence is altered so that the second diagram in Vat. gr. 2249 comes at the end by way of summation. In other manuscripts (e.g., Biblioteca Apostolica Vaticana, Vat. gr. 1787, fol. 136r, of the eleventh century; Biblioteca Apostolica Vaticana, Vat. gr. 504, dated 1105; ms. Coislin 86, fol. 190v, of the twelfth century; and Add. MS. 82952, fol. 14r, of the sixteenth century), the second diagram, which in Vat. gr. 2249 consists of a dichotomy of paired trichotomies, is broken down into three separate diagrams, so that the sequence consists of five, not three, parts – this most likely because the outer margin was not wide enough to accommodate the three-in-one diairesis (Figs. 9–10).

44 For Jacob's ladder in medieval art, see Eva-Maria Kaufmann, Jakobs Traum und der Aufstieg des Menschen zu Gott. Das Thema der Himmelsleiter in der bildenden Kunst des Mittelalters. Tübingen, Berlin 2006.

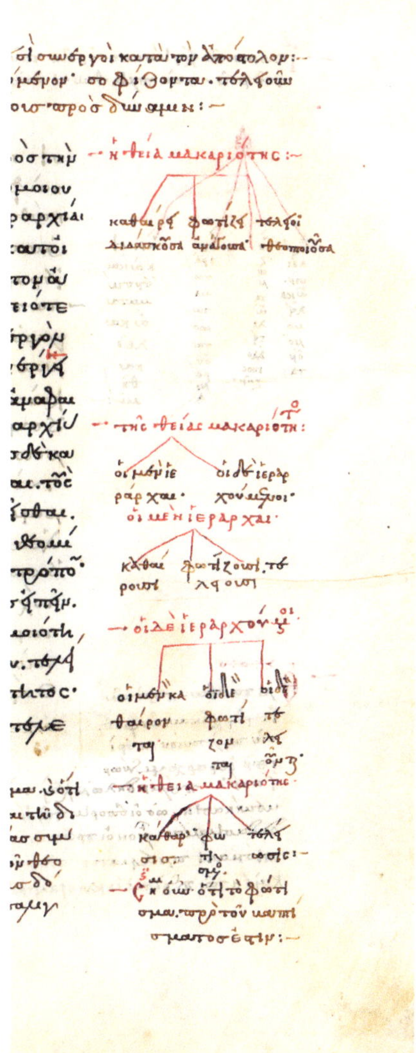

Fig. 9: "Divine Beatitude" and "Purification, Illumination, and Perfection" ('Celestial Hierarchy' 3.2; Greek Diagram 9). Ps.-Dionysius, 'Opera', origin unknown, eleventh century. Biblioteca Apostolica Vaticana, Vat. gr. 1787, fol. 136r (detail). Photo: BAV.

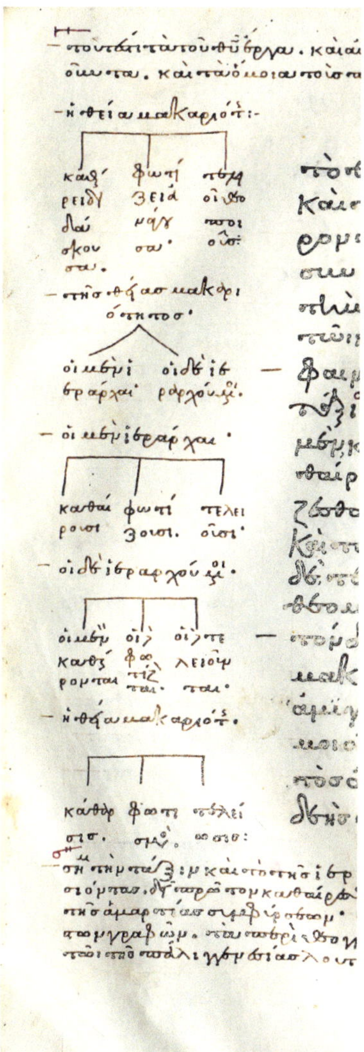

Fig. 10: "Divine Beatitude" and "Purification, Illumination, and Perfection" ('Celestial Hierarchy' 3.2; Greek Diagram 9). Ps.-Dionysius, 'Opera', origin unknown, twelfth century. Paris, Bibliothèque nationale de France, ms. Coislin 86, fol. 190v (detail). Photo: BnF.

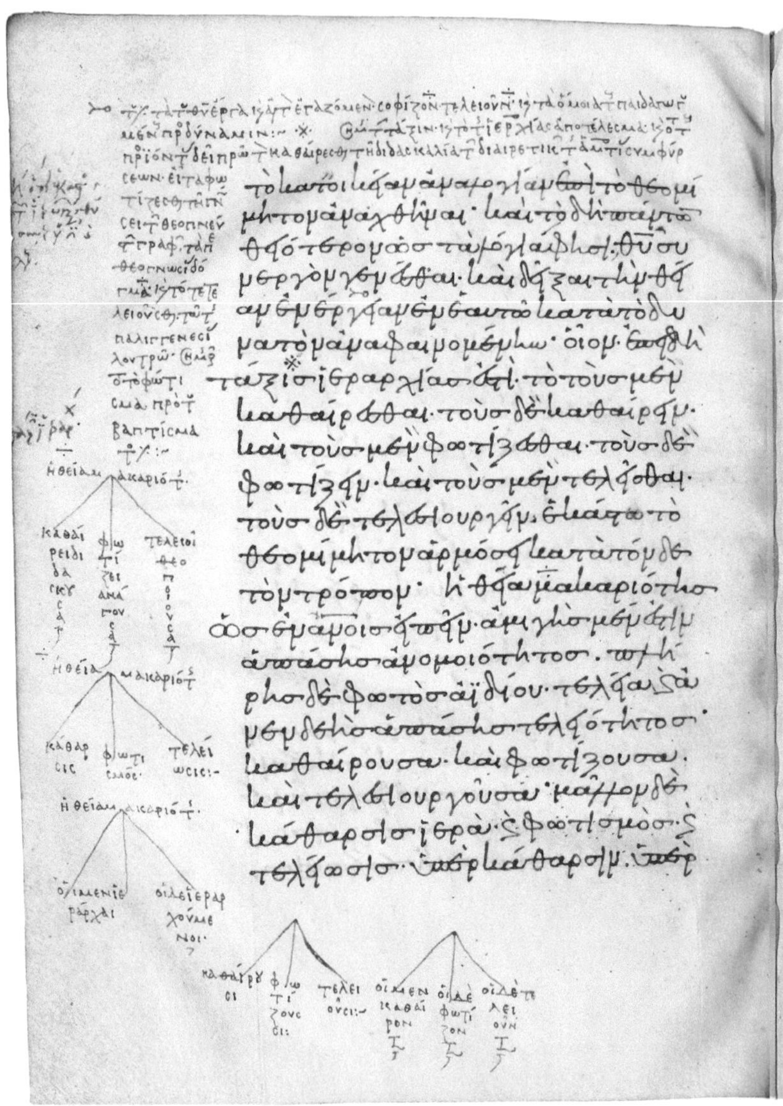

Fig. 11: "Divine Beatitude" and "Purification, Illumination, and Perfection" ('Celestial Hierarchy' 3.2; Greek Diagram 9). Ps.-Dionysius, 'Opera', origin unknown, eleventh century. Paris, Bibliothèque nationale de France, ms. gr. 934, fol. 147v. Photo: BnF.

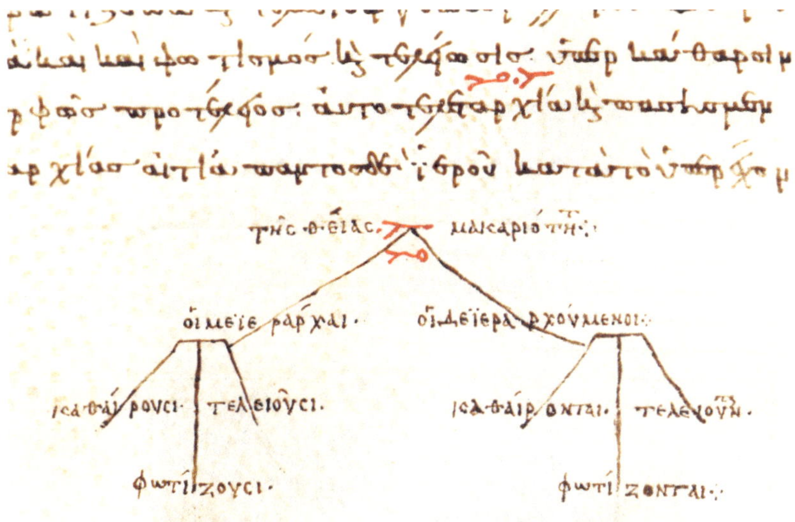

Fig. 12: "Divine Beatitude" and "Purification, Illumination, and Perfection" ('Celestial Hierarchy' 3.2; Greek Diagram 9). Ps.-Dionysius, 'Opera', origin unknown, ninth century. Rome, Biblioteca Vallicelliana, ms. E. 29, fol. 76r (detail). Photo: Biblioteca Vallicelliana.

In several others (Bibliothèque nationale de France, ms. gr. 934, fol. 147v, dating to the eleventh century; and Bibliothèque nationale de France, ms. gr. 439, fol. 14r, dating to the thirteenth century), the dichotomy of the second diagram, in this case placed third in the sequence, was initially drawn as a trichotomy (Fig. 11).

Whereas in some manuscripts, this slip might be attributed to outright error, in others it may simply be the product of mechanical copying. In at least one instance (ms. E. 29, fol. 76r), also from the eleventh century, one can see that the shunting of the second diagram to the third position was undertaken because the lower margin provided enough space for its lateral expansion (Fig. 12).

Whether due to miscomprehension, sloppiness, or experimentation, other manuscripts rework the set more radically. More garbled (or reworked, depending on one's perspective) is the set in ms. B. 55, fol. 24r, an eleventh-century manuscript to which, however, the scholia were added by a later hand (Fig. 13).

In this case the diagram links all five parts of the diagrams for the 'Celestial Hierarchy' 3.2, plus, to conclude, a sixth (a compressed version of the tetrachotomy

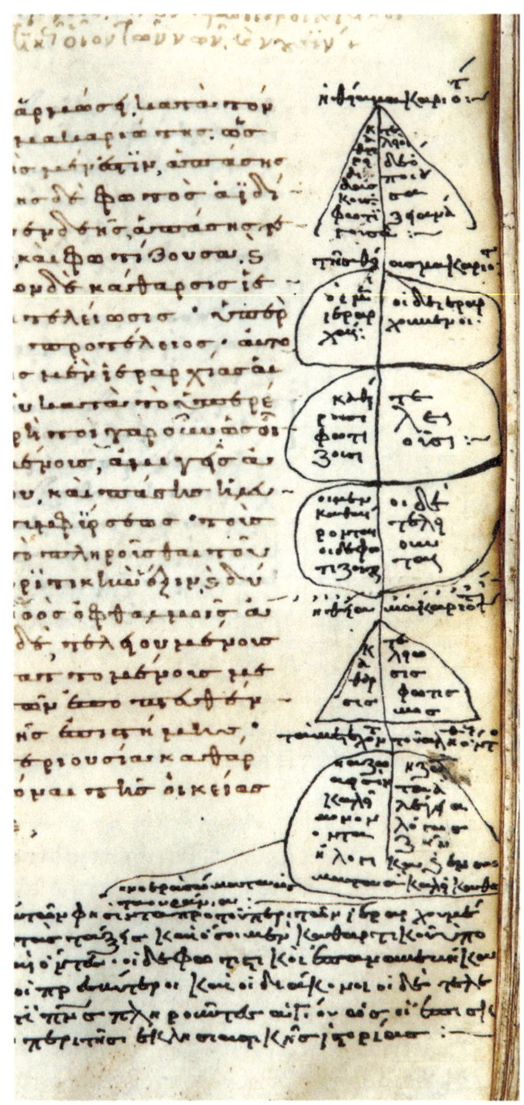

Fig. 13: "Divine Beatitude" and "Purification, Illumination, and Perfection" ('Celestial Hierarchy' 3.2; Greek Diagram 9). Ps.-Dionysius, 'Opera', origin unknown, eleventh century. Rome, Biblioteca Vallicelliana, ms. B. 55, fol. 24r (detail). Photo: Biblioteca Vallicelliana.

for the 'Celestial Hierarchy' 4.2), along a vertical spine that descends the length of the righthand margin. In its overall appearance, the multipart diagram tends to take on the appearance of a tree of Porphyry, in large measure because of the constraints imposed by the margins.[45] Diagrams which might originally have splayed out along a descending diagonal adopted the narrower constraints of the blank space defined by the justification and the edge of the page. The diagram cannot be separated from the material means of its formation and transmission.

**45** The role of margins in rendering the Tree of Porphyry vertical has been underestimated. See Ian Hacking, Trees of Logic, Trees of Porphyry. In: John L. Heilbron (ed.), Advancements of Learning: Essays in Honour of Paolo Rossi. Florence 2007, pp. 221–263; Annemieke R. Verboon, The Medieval Tree of Porphyry. An Organic Structure of Logic. In: Pippa Salonius and Andrea Worm (eds.), The Tree: Symbol, Allegory, and Mnemonic Device in Medieval Art and Thought (International Medieval Research 20). Turnhout 2014, pp. 95–116; and Caterina Tarlazzi, The Latin Tradition of Studying Porphyry's 'Isagoge', ca 800–980. A Working Catalogue of Manuscripts, Glosses and Diagrams. Archives d'histoire doctrinale et littéraire du Moyen Âge 87 (2020), pp. 7–42.

# Figures of Thought

The Neoplatonic philosopher Porphyry (234?–305? C. E.) was perceived as a master of division and the distiller of philosophical tradition. In the words of Boethius,

> [i]t was also Porphyry who acknowledged the utility of [Andronicus of Rhodes'] 'Introduction to the Categories' ['Isagoge'] with reference to this science. For he says that a knowledge of genus, species, difference, property, and accident is a necessary prerequisite to, among several other things, partitioning, which is of the greatest utility.[46]

The visualization of the process of portioning or diairesis described by Porphyry (which only later took on arborial trappings) occurs first, not in manuscripts of the 'Isagoge', whether in Greek or Latin, but rather, as often is the case with such diagrams, in commentaries on it. In this case, the commentary in question is the second and longer of Boethius's two, in which (III.4) diaresis is described in considerable detail, right down to specific individuals (Plato, Cato, and Cicero).[47]

**46** Anicii Manlii Severini Boethii De divisione liber. Critical Edition, Translation, Prolegomena, and Commentary by John Magee. Leiden 1988, p. 5. For Porphyry's 'Isagoge', see Porphyrii Isagoge et In Aristotelis Categorias commentarium. Ed. by Adolf Busse. Berlin 1887; and Porphyre, Isagoge. Ed. and trans. by Alain de Libera and Alain Philippe Segonds. Paris 1998; translated in Porphyry, Introduction. Trans. by Jonathan Barnes. Oxford 2003. For Boethius's commentaries, see Anicii Manlii Severini Boethii In Isagogen Porphyrii Commenta. Ed. by Samuel Brandt. Vienna, Leipzig 1906; and Aristoteles Latinus, I, 1–5, Categoriae vel Praedicamenta. Ed. by Lorenzo Minio-Paluello (Corpus philosophorum Medii Aevi). Bruges 1961. There was a substantial Neoplatonic critique of Aristotle's 'Categories'; see Richard Sorabji, The Philosophy of the Commentators 200–600 AD. A Sourcebook, vol. 3: Logic & Metaphysics. London 2004, pp. 56–125.

**47** In Isagogen Porphyrii Commenta (note 46), p. 208: *Substantia igitur generalissimum genus est; haec enim de cunctis aliis praedicatur. Ac primum huius species duae, corporeum, incorporeum; nam et quod corporeum est, substantia dicitur et item quod incorporeum est, substantia praedicatur. Sub corporeo vero animatum atque inanimatum corpus ponitur, sub animato corpore animal ponitur; nam si sensibile adicias animato corpori, animal facis, reliqua vero pars, id est species, continet animatum insensibile corpus. Sub animali autem rationale atque irrationale, sub rationali homo atque deus; nam si rationali mortale subieceris, hominem feceris, si immortale, deum, deum vero corporeum; hunc enim mundum ueteres deum vocabant et Iovis eum appellatione dignati sunt deumque solem caeteraque caelestia corpora, quae animata esse cum Plato, tum plurimus doctorum chorus arbitratus est. Sub homine vero individui singularesque homines ut Plato, Cato, Cicero et caeteri, quorum numerum pluralitas infinita non recipit. Cuius rei subiecta descriptio sub oculos ponat exemplum: incorporea corpus animatum | inanimatum animatum corpus sensibile | insensibile animal rationale | irrationale rationale animal mortale | immortale homo | Plato Cato Cicero.*

Although predicated on the Aristotelian categories, the Tree of Porphyry is also Platonic in conception or at least easily adapted to a Platonic scheme of things. The inversion represented by the Tree, which, unlike a sapling planted in the earth, 'grows' downward from the most general genus or God, was perfectly suited to the expression of a Platonized worldview predicated on participation.[48] A diagram in a tenth-century copy of the 'Categoriae decem' (Biblioteca Apostolica Vaticana, Pal. lat. 213, fol. 22r), a popular fourth-century summary of Aristotle's 'Categories' commonly, if inaccurately, attributed to Augustine, grants *OIVCIA* ('Being' or 'Substance') spelled in majuscule letters at the top, the prominence it deserves in this scheme of things (Fig. 14).[49]

Once again, the diagram accompanies a commentary (specifically, a prologue), an indication that diagrams and diagrammatic thinking formed an essential constituent of the mental apparatus that readers brought to the text. From its summit, where, by way of defining *ousia* a separate hand added *Generalissimum* below *Genus*, the diagram descends to its second level (*Secundus gradus*), in this case, animals (although another annotator adds *genera* indicating that this is but one example of many). From here the diagram descends again to the specific species (*Species specialis*) of man, followed by the individual, Cicero, a *species specialissima*. All these labels follow the 'Categoriae decem' IX.58:

> The second ousiai are called, genus and species, that is, animal and man. He [Aristotle] therefore says that these are called 'second substances' because that which is neither in the subject nor predicated of the subject is more important.

**48** A metaphor that was to have a long afterlife; see A. B. Chambers, 'I was But an Inverted Tree'. Notes Toward the History of an Idea. Studies in the Renaissance 8 (1961), pp. 291–299; Maria Luisa Gatti, 'Celestial Plants with the Roots Up There'. A Metaphor of the Human Existence in 'Timaeus' of Plato. Rivista di filosofia neoscolastica 107 (2015), pp. 111–118; and José Higuera Rubio, The Evolution of Relational Tree-Diagrams from the Twelfth to Fourteenth Century. Visual Devices and Models of Knowledge. In: Michael D. Bintley and Pippa Salonius (eds.), Trees as Symbol and Metaphor in the Middle Ages: Comparative Contexts. Cambridge 2024, pp. 132–153, at pp. 149–153.

**49** For the 'Categoriae decem', see John Marenbom, From the Circle of Alcuin to the School of Auxerre. Logic, Theology and Philosophy in the Early Middle Ages. Cambridge 1981, and 'Les dix catégories', ou, 'Paraphrase thémistienne', du Pseudo-Augustin. Texte légèrement émendé de l'édition de L. Minio-Paluello. Ed. and trans. by Alain Galonnier (Philosophes médiévaux 70). Louvain-la-Neuve 2021, pp. 1–5 and Categoriae vel Praedicamenta. Ed. by Lorenzo Minio-Paluello (Corpus philosophorum Medii Aevi). Bruges 1961, pp. 133–175.

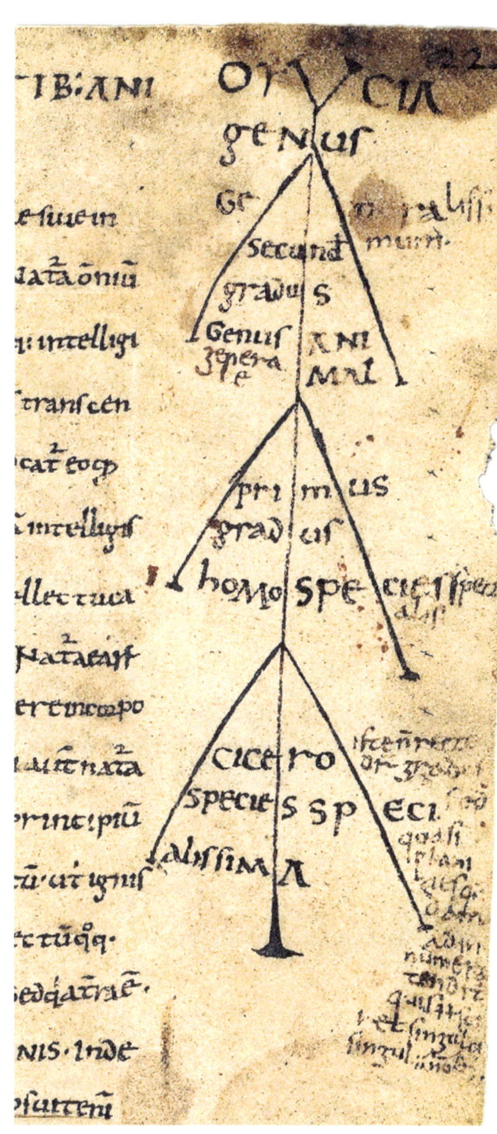

Fig. 14: Tree of Porphyry. 'Categoriae decem', etc., northern France, tenth century. Biblioteca Apostolica Vaticana, Pal. lat. 213, fol. 22r (detail). Photo: BAV.]

> "Second substances" are therefore called genus and species because they alone indicate the first.[50]

Elsewhere (IX.60), the same chapter argues that "of the secondary substances themselves, the species is more important than the genus, for the species is closer to the substance than the genus".[51] The only respect in which the diagram departs from the text is the substitution of Cicero for Socrates, of whom it is said (IX.60): "if one wished to speak about Socrates without saying his name it would signify him more if one said 'man' than if one said 'animal' (for we can recognize both a horse and an eagle as an 'animal')."[52]

Variants of some diagrams to the Dionysian corpus lend their implicit spatialization of hierarchy the explicit trappings of architecture. For example, the 'Ecclesiastical Hierarchy' 2.3.6 unpacks the metaphor of holy athleticism at considerable length as part of its drawn-out discussion of the rite of baptism:[53]

> Now you may perceive the distinct images of these things [the more perfect mysteries of the supreme Godhead] in the religious rites performed by the hierarch. For the godlike hierarch starts with the holy anointing, but the priest under him complete the divine service of the chrism, summoning the initiated, in type, to the holy contests within which he is placed under Christ as umpire (since as God he is framer of the laws of contest); as wise, he placed its laws; but as generous, he fixed the awards suitable to the victors. And this is yet more divine, inasmuch as being generous, he entered the lists with them, contending, on behalf of their freedom and victory against the power of death and destruction, he who is initiated will enter the contests as those of God rejoicing.[54]

**50** Les dix catégories (note 49) IX.58, p. 186: *Secundae dicuntur usiae genus et species, id est animal et homo. Has ergo ‚secundas substantias' nominari dicit propterea quod illa sit potior quae neque in subiecto est neque de subiecto praedicatur. Secundae autem substantiae idcirco dictae sunt genus et species quod solae indicent primam.*

**51** Ibid., p. 188: *Ipsarum deinde secundarum usiarum potior est species genere; magis enim proxima est species primac usiae quam genus.*

**52** Ibid.: *Ut, si quis Socraten uolens dicere, omisso eius nomine, magis eum significet si 'hominem' dixerit quam si 'animal' ('animal' enim et equum et aquilam possumus agnoscere).*

**53** For the metaphorics of holy athleticism, see Richard H. Blum, The Sacred Athlete. On the Mystical Experience and Dionysius, its Westernworld Fountainhead. Langham MD 1991.

**54** Corpus Dionysiacum (note 36), vol. 2, p. 77.8–17; The Celestial and Ecclesiastical Hierarchy (note 36), p. 59.

Christ, the archetypal athlete, awards the ultimate prize, which is divinization, whose basis and precondition, however, is the baptismal rite. The accompanying diagram reduces the passage as follows:

*ὁ Χριστός* (partially trimmed) ("Christ")
*ὡς μὲν θεός, ἀθλοθετεῖ* ("as God, he serves as the umpire")
*ὡς δὲ σοφὸς, νομοθετεῖ* ("as wise, places its laws [i.e., legislates]")
*ὡς καλὸς καλλύνει τὰ ἆθλα* ("as beautiful, fixes the awards")
*ὡς ἀγαθὸς συναγωνίζεται* ("as good, struggles alongside")

In most manuscripts, the diairesis diagram takes the form of a simple tetrachotomy (e.g., in Vat. gr. 2249, fol. 103v). In one manuscript (Bibliothèque nationale de France, ms. gr. 446, fol. 183v), however, dating to the fifteenth century, the diagram assumes figural form; a half-length figure of Christ, his arms extended in blessing, occupies a semicircular space reminiscent of the conch of an apse from which extend four ray-like extensions, thereby evoking the setting in which baptism would take place and to which it allowed entry (Fig. 15).[55]

In this case, we see a relatively rare example of a phenomenon far more common in the Latin West, namely, the introduction of figural imagery into the space of the diagram, which has the effect of lending the abstract concepts it presents concrete animation and embodiment.[56]

**55** For the impact of Dionysian ideas on church decoration and the structuring of their spaces, see Francesca Dell'Acqua and Ernesto Sergio Mainoldi (eds.), Pseudo-Dionysius and Christian Visual Culture, c. 500–900. New Approaches to Byzantine History and Culture. London, New York 2020. See also by Pauli Annala, From the Exterior to the Interior, and Beyond. Spiritual Topography in St Maximus' 'Mystagogia'. In: Antoine Lévy et al. (eds.), The Architecture of the Cosmos. St Maximus Confessor. New Perspectives. Helsinki 2015, pp. 279–297, at pp. 279–280. As pointed out to me by Herbert Kessler, the motif of the half-length Christ surmounting the diagram is also reminiscent of representations of him atop the ladder in illustrations to John Climacus's 'Scala paradisi', for which see John Martin, The Illustration of the Heavenly Ladder of John Climacus (Studies in Manuscript Illumination 5). Princeton 1954; and Ravinder Binning, The Memory Prison. Carceral and Sacred Space in an Ekphrasis by John Climacus. Dumbarton Oaks Papers 76 (2022), pp. 9–30. Although in the diagram the rays representing the four parts of the diairesis descend from Christ, and in the Heavenly Ladder the monk ascends the rungs of the ladder, both images characterize the ascetic's accomplishment of Christ-like virtue in terms of a struggle defined in terms of reciprocal up-and-down movement.

**56** For Byzantine diagrams, see Linda Safran, A Prolegomenon to Byzantine Diagrams. In: Marcia Kupfer, Adam Cohen and J. H. (Yossi) Chajes (eds.), The Visualization of Knowledge in Medieval and Early Modern Europe (Studies in the Visual Cultures of the Middle Ages 16). Turnhout 2020, pp. 361–382; and ead., Byzantine Diagrams. In: Jeffrey F. Hamburger, David Roxburgh and Linda Safran (eds.), The Diagram as Paradigm: Medieval Diagrams in a Cross-Cultural Perspective (Byzantine, Western European, and Islamicate). Washington DC 2022, pp. 13–32.

Fig. 15: "Christ" ('Ecclesiastical Hierarchy' 2.3.6; Greek Diagram 15). Ps.-Dionysius, 'Opera', origin unknown, 1348. Paris, Bibliothèque nationale de France, ms. gr. 446, fol. 183v (detail). Photo: BnF.

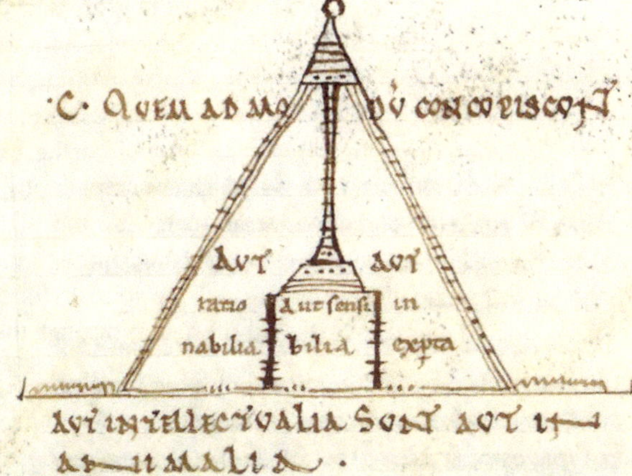

Fig. 16: "Those Things which long for the Good" ('Divine Names' 4.2; Latin Diagram 21). Ps.-Dionysius, 'Opera', Mont-Saint-Michel, 1080–1100. Avranches, Bibliothèque municipale Edouard Le Héricher, ms. 47, 120v (detail). Photo: CNRS-IRHT.

At least one manuscript of John Scottus Eriugena's translation of the Dionysian corpus (a twelfth-century manuscript from Mont-Saint-Michel, Avranches, Bibliothèque municipale Edouard Le Héricher, ms. 47, fol. 120v), applies architectural elements to the diagram for the 'Divine Names' 4.2, a passage that, especially as distilled by the diagram, reads like a transposition of Plato's Analogy of the Sun and Divided Line ('Republic' 507b–509c; 509d–511e) (Fig. 16):

> Whatever pertains to the heavenly hierarchy is from the good: the purifications which are suitable for angels, their super-cosmic illumination, and the complete working out of the whole angelic perfection. [...] After these sacred and holy intellects come the souls and all of their goods. That they are the intellects that they are, that they have an essential and indestructible life, are also due to the goodness beyond good; even their being itself is possible through their power to be raised up to the angelic life. [...] Further, if it is necessary to say anything concerning irrational souls (living beings) – those which fly in the air or are held to the earth, those animals in water (those which are amphibious), and those which live buried in the earth and are covered by it – it is this: all those which have a sensible soul or life are besouled or enlivened through the good. All plants have their growing and moving life through the good. Indeed, all soulless and lifeless being is and receives its essential conditions through the good.[57]

Where Dionysius expands on the 'Republic', however, is in extending the participation in the Good to all living things. Although separate from creation, the Good, fulfilling a role comparable to that of Plato's Demiurge as described in the 'Timaeus', informs all aspects of creation, just as by way of comparison the light of the sun informs all forms of being according to its capacity to receive it.

In both its Greek and Latin versions (of which the latter is reproduced here), the diagrammatic synopsis of this passage reads as follows:

*Quae bonum concupiscent* ("Those things which long for the Good")
*Aut rationalibilia* ("Whether rational")
*Aut sensibilia* ("Or things that perceive through the senses")
*Aut inexperta* ("Or without a share in")
*Aut intellectualia sunt* ("Or they are intelligible things")
*Aut animalia* ("Or animals")

**57** Corpus Dionysiacum (note 36), vol. 1, pp. 145.4–146.5; John D. Jones, Pseudo-Dionysius Areopagite, The Divine Name and The Mystical Theology. Translated from the Greek with an Introductory Study (Mediaeval Philosophical Texts in Translation 21). Milwaukee WI 2015, pp. 134–135.

In most of the early Latin manuscripts (tenth and eleventh century), the diagram transforms a fivefold diairesis into what looks like an omega with an added central vertical placed within two converging diagonals. In this form the diagram bears an uncanny resemblance to the monogram of Alpha and Omega, a common graphic device in the art of the early Western Middle Ages connoting temporal and cosmic completeness (Ap 22.13; "I am Alpha and Omega, the first and the last, the beginning and the end"). If intended, the allusion would have provided an appropriate emblem of the very phenomenon Dionysius wishes to describe, the unity of the cosmos suffused by the Good (cf. 'Divine Names' 4.4: "[The good is the cause] of the periodic return from the same place into the same place of the two luminaries, which the writings call 'great', according to which our days, nights, months, and years are measured and determined").[58] In the manuscript from Mont-Saint-Michel, however, the monogram-like form is transformed into a pyramidal structure with a central supporting column (not unlike some of the spaces at the abbey), the division of whose base attaches the three terms it defines, not to lines, but rather to the spaces they create. In this instance, figure and ground signify simultaneously. Just as the schematic plans used to lay out pictorial programs within architectural space assumed diagrammatic form, so too diagrams could take on the trappings of architecture to articulate and amplify their meaning using metaphors of edification.[59]

**58** Jones (note 57), p. 135.
**59** From the twelfth century on, diagrams adopt far more elaborate architectural forms. For an elaborate example of a medieval plan for a program of wall paintings within a vaulted space, see Ludovico V. Geymonat, Un disegno preparatorio del XIII secolo per un ciclo pittorico sull'Apocalisse. Ikon 6 (2013), pp. 55–64; also, more generally, Ludovico Geymonat, Paolo Piva and Fabio Scirea, Pittura murale, contesto strutturale, pianificazione iconografica (esempi del XIII secolo). In: Paolo Piva (ed.), L'arte medievale nel contesto (300–1300). Funzione, iconografia, techniche (Di fronte e attraverso 635; Storia dell'arte 27). Milan 2006, pp. 501–532.

# The Athletic Scholar

A leap to the sixteenth century, in particular to Charles Bovelles (c. 1475–1566), takes us from the beginnings of the Dionysian tradition in late antiquity to its renaissance in the early modern period.[60] A student of Jacques Lefèvre d'Étaples, who had overseen the revision and printing of a second edition of Traversari's translation of Dionysius, published in Paris on 6th February 1498 (i.e., 1499 according to the modern calendar), Bovelles, a canon of Noyon Cathedral, published prolifically on subjects ranging from mathematics, theoretical and practical, to religion and philosophy.[61] His publications reveal an obsession with diagrams, and not only for pedagogic reasons. Familiar from his teacher with the writings not only of Ramon Llull, of whom he wrote the first biography (1511), but also of Nicholas of Cusa, Bovelles likewise made mathematics a cornerstone of his philosophical and religious writings, using it to demonstrate, not merely illustrate, his ideas.[62] From Cusa, Bovelles inherited a fascination with negative theology expressed in terms

**60** See Joseph M. Victor, Charles de Bovelles 1479–1553. An Intellectual Biography (Travaux d'Humanisme et Renaissance 161). Geneva 1978. Although they are frequently reproduced, Bovelles's diagrams are seldom analyzed in detail. Anne-Hélène Klinger-Dollé, Le 'De Sensu' de Charles de Bovelles (1511). Conception philosophique des sens et figuration de la pensée (Travaux d'Humanism et Renaissance 557). Geneva 2016, represents a notable exception. See also Rebecca E. Zorach, Meditation, Idolatry, Mathematics. The Printed Image in Europe Around 1500. In: Michael W. Cole and Rebecca E. Zorach (eds.), The Idol in the Age of Art. Objects, Devotions, and the Early Modern World. Farnham 2009, pp. 317–342.

**61** For Bovelles's mathematics, see Robert J. Oosterhout, Reading and Numerology in the Early French Reform. Reformation & Renaissance Review 24 (2022), pp. 44–72, and for the Dionysian current in his thought, culminating in the 'Liber divinae caliginis' (1526), see Pierre Magnard, Charles de Bovelles, penseur dionysien. In: Stéphanie Toussaint and Christian Trottmann (eds.), Le Pseudo-Denys à la Renaissance. Actes du colloque Tours, 27–29 mai 2010. Paris 2014, pp. 196–208.

**62** For Bovelles and Llullism, see Victor (note 60), pp. 57–71; Jordi Gaya, Réminiscences lulliennes dans l'anthropologie de Bovelles. In: Charles de Bovelles en son cinquième centenaire 1479–1979. Actes du colloque international tenu à Noyon les 14–16 septembre 1979. Paris 1982, pp. 143–156; and Linda Báez Rubí, Lullism Among French and Spanish Humanists of the Early 16th Century. In: Amy M. Austin (ed.), A Companion to Ramon Llull and Llullism (Brill's Companions to the Christian Tradition 82). Leiden, Boston 2018, pp. 397–436. For his debt to Cusa, see Maurice de Gandillac, Lefèvre d'Étaples et Charles de Bouelles, lecteurs de Nicolas de Cues. In: Colloque International de Tours (XIVe stage). L'humanisme français au début de la Renaissance. Paris 1973, pp. 155–171; and Jocelyne Sfez, Charles de Bovelles face à l'heritage cusain. In: Anne-Hélène Klinger-Dollé and Emmanuel Faye (eds.), Charles de Bovelles. Philosophe et pedagogue, suivi de Oposcule métaphysique de Charles de Bovelles (1504). Paris 2021, pp. 19–46.

of mathematics; from Llull, a lifelong preoccupation with, first, human nature as a microcosm of the macrocosm and, second, nature itself as a *scala entis* which man could ascend to God.[63] For Bovelles, as for Dionysius, ontology and epistemology were essentially one. Where Bovelles departs from Dionysian precedent is in the degree to which for him the realm of symbols, which for Dionysius remained, above all else, the dissimilar likenesses supplied by scripture, has been supplanted by the Book of Nature perceived directly by the senses. For Bovelles, book learning is not so much the starting point of a process of ascent leading to divinity as it is the outflowing of the mind, which stands as the nexus between the human and the divine.

In Bovelles's 'Liber de sensu', the disposition of branching diagrams encompasses the greatest enlargement of space conceivable, that of the entire cosmos. The book begins with a division of the senses (*Sensus divisio*) that links inner and outer worlds: "One of the senses is external, another internal. The exterior [sense] is located on the surface of the human body, exposed to the larger world. The interior, however, is hidden within, and is the sense of the smaller world".[64] In this there is nothing new; in his 'Etymologies' XI.i.6, Isidore of Seville states as much with his customary economy, "[b]ut man is double, interior and exterior. The inner man, the soul, the outer man, the body".[65] Less customary, however, is Bovelles's visualization of this ancient formula in one of three full-page diagrams, in this case serving as a summary at the end of the treatise (Fig. 17):

**63** For Bovelles and negative theology, see Jan Miernowski, Le dieu néant. Théologie negatives à l'aube des temps modernes (Studies in the History of Christian Thought 82). Leiden, New York, 1998, pp. 71–89. For mathematics as the cornerstone of philosophical inquiry in Bovelles (a Cusan inheritance), see Angela Axworthy, Le statut épistémologique de la géométrie d'après l'Introductio in Geometriam' de Charles de Bovelles. In: Anne-Hélène Klinger-Dollé and Emmanuel Faye (eds.), Charles de Bovelles: Philosophe et pedagogue, suivi de Opuscule métaphysique de Charles de Bovelles (1504). Paris 2021, pp. 101–119. For Bovelles on the microcosm, see Tamara Albertini, Der Mikrokosmos-Topos als Denkfigur der Analogie in der Renaissance aufgezeigt an der Philosophie Charles de Bovelles. In: Karen Gloy and Manuel Bachmann (eds.), Das Analogiedenken. Vorstösse in ein neues Gebiet der Rationalitätstheorie (Alber Reihe Philosophie). Freiburg i. Br. 2000, pp. 184–212.

**64** Que hoc volumine (Caroli Bovilli) continentur: Liber de intellectu etc., fol. 22r: *Sensuum alius est exterior, alius interior. Exterior in humani corporis superficie situs est, maiori mundo expositus. Interior vero intus abditus est, & minoris mundo sensus.*

**65** Isidori Hispalensis Episcopi, Etymologiarum sive Originum libri XX. Ed. by Wallace M. Lindsay. Oxford 1911, vol. 2, p. 15: *Duplex est autem homo, interior et exterior. Interior homo, anima, exterior homo, corpus.*

Fig. 17: The Athletic Scholar. Charles de Bovelles, *Que hoc volumine continentur*: […] *Liber de sensu* […], Paris, Henri Estienne, 1510, fol. 60v. Paris, Bibliothèque nationale de France, RES-R-155. Photo: BnF.

The image also provides a tangible as well as a visible cue to how the book should be read.[66] The active scholar, literally, studious, athletic (*Studiosus Palestrites*) – a variation on the early Christian topos of the monk as an athlete of virtue (the same metaphor employed by Dionysius to characterize the baptismal rite) – employs all five senses to engage with the world around him but also, no less important, to use the world as a stepping-stone to heavenly things, indicated by the stars that occupy his thoughts. The exterior world becomes the interior world, which in turn contains the entire empyrean. The scholar accomplishes this omniscient concordance of outer and inner through writing and reading, represented by the actions of his left and right hands, of which the former, embodying the sense of touch, grasps an open book that is itself illustrated with diagrams.[67] In the words of the superscription,

> Quid agat studiosus palestrites
> Scribimus & legimus: loquimur, meditamur in aures
> Quod cadit: His quinis omnia discit homo.
> Auribus: ore, oculis, manibus, cerebroque cietur.
> Qui cupit etheros doctus adire polos[68]

In essence, Bovelles's image charts a circulation according to which sensory experience informs the intellect but in which the mind in turn manifests its ideas in auditory, visible, and palpable form through speech, script, and publication. Chains linking the frontal figure's mouth to his ears signal the interconnection between speech (*locutio*) and hearing (*auditio*), which, in a gesture to logocentricity and the perceived simplicity of sound, receives pride of place.[69] Crowning the scholar's cranium is Imagination.[70] Nicholas of Cusa's notion of *the coincidentia oppositorum* – the subject of the fourth treatise in the compendium to which 'De sensu' belongs

**66** See Guido Giglioni, La natura impara a leggere e scrivere. Mente, mano e mono del 'Liber de Sensu' di Charles de Bovelles. Bruniana & Campanelliana 24 (2018), pp. 447–450.
**67** On the Renaissance rehabilitation of the sense of touch, see Anna Corrias, Senses, Outer. In: Encyclopedia of Renaissance Philosophy (2022), cols. 2981–2983.
**68** Paris, Bibliothèque nationale de France, RES-R-155, fol. 60v: "What should the student-athlete do? We write and read; we speak, we meditate on what falls upon the ears. Through these five, man learns all things: he is stirred by ears, mouth, eyes, hands, and brain, who desires, as a learned man, to ascend to the ethereal heavens."
**69** On the superiority of sound, see Anna Corrias, When the Eyes are Shut. The Strange Case of Girolamo Cardano's Idolum in 'Somniorum Synesiorum Libri IIII' (1562). Journal of the History of Ideas 79 (2018), pp. 179–197.
**70** See Michele Merlicco, The Role of Imagination in Charles de Bovelles 'Liber de sensu'. Bruniana & Campanelliana 24 (2018), pp. 461–474.

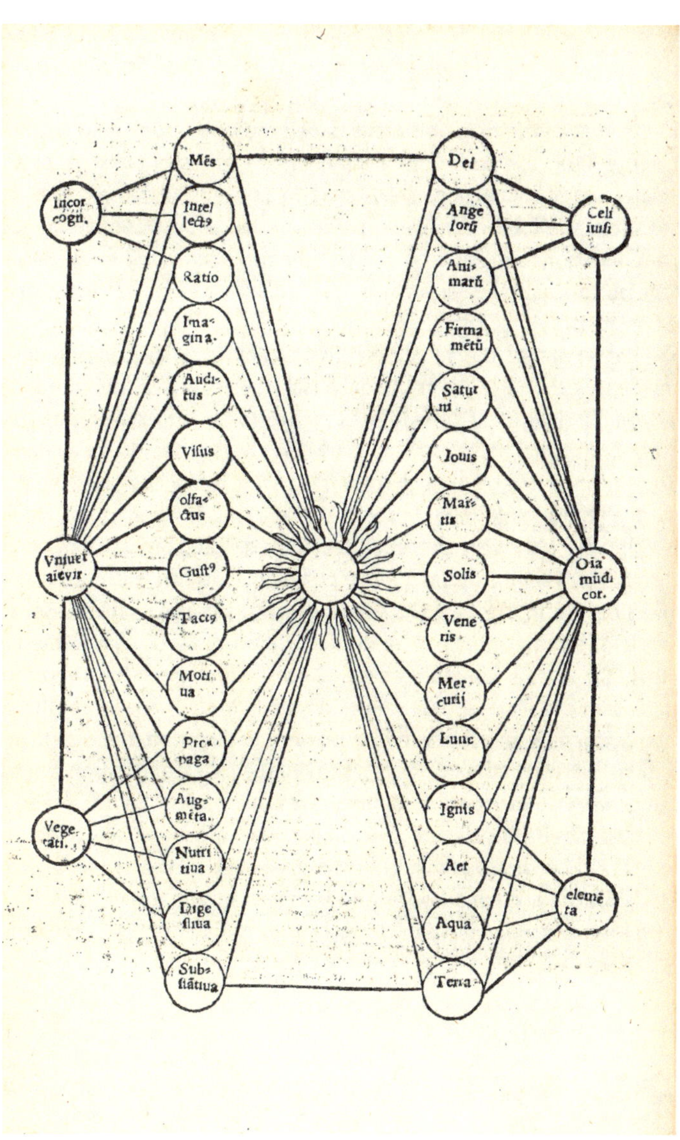


Fig. 18: Correlation of the Subjective and Objective Worlds. Charles de Bovelles, *Que hoc volumine continentur*: [...] *Liber de sensu* [...], Paris, Henri Estienne, 1510, fol. 42v. Photo: BnF.

and a principle with which Bovelles would have been intimately familiar, having assisted Jacques Lefèvre d'Étaples over many years with his 'Opera omnia' edition of the cardinal's work, published in 1514 – here receives new meaning.

From the look of the diagrams on its pages, the open book held by the active scholar is the 'Liber de sensu' itself. One of its many diagrams traces a highly differentiated set of connections predicated on a systematic framework of subject-object relations, defined here as the correspondence between human faculties, senses, and functions, ranging from mind at the top (*mens*) to Substance (*substantiva*) at the bottom, and the hierarchy of the cosmos, with God at the top and Earth at the opposite pole (Fig. 18).[71]

At the center stands the sun, linked to and animating all components of the diagram, identified on the left as the universal powers of the soul (the subjective side) and, on the right, as all the bodies of the world (the objective side). Bovelles's intellectual if not literal heliocentricity marks man as the measure of all things.[72] As if in a pop-up book, the diagram unfolds from a horizontal line bisecting the page from which all things unfold. In a conceit that is as much visual as it is intellectual, thereby embodying the very concept it seeks to explicate; the space of the cosmos and man's place within it opens before our eyes. The first eleven terms on the righthand side are in the genitive as opposed to the nominative case, so that, for example, the uppermost pair reads "The Mind of God", that at the bottom, Substantives (i.e., things that merely exist) / Earth. Excluding this lowermost row, the diagram divides the scale of the faculties on the left into three levels: the vegetative at the bottom (associated with four powers ranging from the digestive to the propagative), paired on the opposite side with the four elements, and, at the top, the three powers of incorporeal cognition (reason, intellect, mind), linked on the right side with Souls, Angels, and God, collectively identified as constituting the invisible heaven. On the left, the middle ranks are filled by the five senses, to which are added, bottom and top, Motion and Imagination, and, on the right, by seven planets (the sun and moon included), to which, for symmetry's sake, the firmament is added.

**71** The classic essay on the topic of subject-object relations in the Renaissance remains Ernst Cassirer, The Individual and the Cosmos in Renaissance Philosophy. Trans. by Mario Domandi. New York 1963, pp. 123–191.

**72** For the "heliocentricity" of fifteenth- and sixteenth-century hermetic Neoplatonism, see Frances A. Yates, Giordano Bruni and the Hermetic Tradition. London 1964, pp. 151–155.

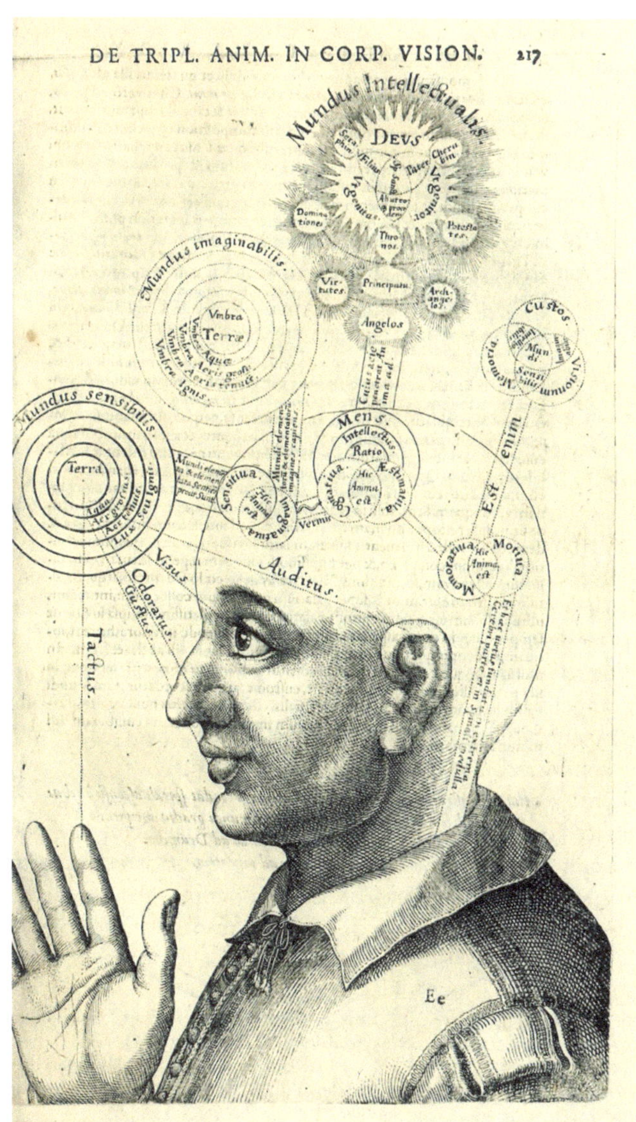


Fig. 19: Robert Fludd, 'Utriusque cosmi', Oppenheim: Johan-Theodori de Bry, 1617–1621, vol. 1, p. 217. Photo: archive.org.

Bovelles's construct of self and cosmos as mirror images of one another also echoes Nicholas of Cusa – and anticipates Robert Fludd's magnum opus 'Utriusque Cosmi, Maioris scilicet et Minoris, metaphysica, physica, atque technica Historia' (The Metaphysical, Physical, and Technical History of the Two Worlds, Namely the Greater and the Lesser), published in Oppenheim between 1617 and 1621 (Fig. 19).[73] As Cusa states in 'De coniecturis',

> For the more subtly the mind contemplates itself in and through the world unfolded from itself, the more abundantly fruitful it is made within itself, since its End is Infinite Reason. Only in Infinite Reason will the mind behold itself as it is; and Infinite Reason alone is the Rational Measure for all things.[74]

Not only does the infinite contain the finite, but the finite also contains the infinite, in essence, an expression of Neoplatonic, specifically Dionysian hierarchy. The correlation between mind and world expressed in terms of a threefold hierarchy of cognition is Dionysian as well: sensory perception, rational understanding, and intellectual intuition, of which the latter, as in Bovelles's reflection on Cusa, is tantamount to unity with God.[75]

In its perspectival conception of the relationship between the self and the world, Bovelles's construction seems very modern. In other respects, however, it proves very medieval. His diagrams can be compared with the image of man as the microcosm attached to a set of glossaries, among them, the 'Glossarium Salomonis', part of a compendium (Munich, Bayerische Staatsbibliothek, Clm 13002, fol. 7v) written at Prüfening outside of Regensburg in 1158 but augmented with illustrations shortly afterwards, in 1165 (Fig. 20).

Inscriptions extending from the figure's extremities and body parts define his relationship to the natural world, constituted by the four elements in the corners of the composition, Fire and Air at top left and right, associated respectively with sight, hearing, and smell; Water and Earth at the bottom, with taste and touch. The halo-like circle around his head, which inevitably reads as an allusion to Christ, is

**73** See Jeffrey F. Hamburger, 'The Triple Essence of the Visual Process', or Thinking with Diagrams in the Middle Ages and Modernity. Codex Aquilarensis 37 (2021), pp. 41–77.
**74** Nicolai de Cusa Opera Omnia, vol. 3: De Coniecturis. Ed. by Josef Koch, Karl Bormann and Hans Gerhard Senger. Hamburg 1972, I.1.5; Nicholas of Cusa, De Coniecturis (On Surmises). Trans. by Jasper Hopkins (Metaphysical Speculations 2). Minneapolis 2000, p. 165.
**75** See Ulrich Hedtke, *Coincidentia oppositorum* oder die weltliche Unendlichkeit. Dialektik und Systemdenken bei Nikolaus von Kues. In: Helga Bergmann (ed.), Dialektik und Systemdenken. Historische Aspekte. Nikolaus von Kues, franz. Aufklärung, Schelling. Berlin 1977, pp. 19–54.

Fig. 20: Man as the Microcosm. 'Glossarium Salomonis', Prüfening, 1158/1165. Munich, Bayerische Staatsbibliothek, Clm 13002, fol. 7v (detail). Photo: BSB.

inscribed *Instar celestis spherae* ("Like the celestial sphere"). Six spokes connect the man's sense organs to this sphere: sun and moon emanate from the eyes; Jupiter and Mercury from the ears; and Mars and Venus from the nostrils. A seventh spoke, identified as Saturn, links the mouth to Air and the production of sound, whether wind or thunder, all associations drawn from Honorius Augustodunensis's 'Imago mundi'. Part of a series of images which includes illustrations of anatomy and cauterization as well as allegories of the Virtues and Vices, the image both brings the body very much down to earth yet elevates it in relation to the heavens.

Bovelles's image of the *studiosus palestrites* provides a fitting point at which to conclude this discussion of the spatial dimensions of medieval diagrams. From the space carved out by diaresis diagrams within the confines of the codex, diagrams expanded their purview over the course of the Middle Ages to take in the whole of God's creation, to the point that the *Deus artifex* himself could be conceived of as having configured the cosmos with a compass.[76] Medieval spaces of knowledge encompassed not only the confines of libraries or the extended social networks within which books were written, exchanged, and read; they also took shape on the page, most persuasively in the form of diagrams.[77]

**76** See John Lowden, The Making of the Bible Moralisées, 2 vols. University Park PA 2000, vol. 1, pp. 47–50 and 87–88; idem, The Holkham Bible Picture Book and the Bible Moralisée. In: James H. Marrow, Richard A Linenthal and William Noel (eds.), The Medieval Book: Glosses from Friends & Colleagues of Christopher de Hamel. 't Goy-Houten 2020, pp. 75–83; and Antonia Martínez Ruipérez, The Moral Compass and Mortal Slumber. Divine and Human Reason in the 'Bibles Moralisées'. Journal of the Warburg and Courtauld Institutes 81 (2018), pp. 1–33.
**77** The disposition of text on the page, especially in glossed books, itself constitutes a spatial organization of knowledge; see Malcolm B. Parkes, The Influence of the Concepts of *ordinatio* and *compilatio* on the Development of the Book. In: Jonathan J. G. Alexander and Margaret T. Gibson (eds.), Medieval Learning and Literature. Essays Presented to Richard William Hunt. Oxford 1976, pp. 115–141; and Lesley Smith, Biblical Gloss and Commentary. The Scaffolding of Scripture. In: Marcia Kupfer, Adam Cohen and J. H. (Yossi) Chajes (eds.), The Visualization of Knowledge in Medieval and Early Modern Europe (Studies in the Visual Cultures of the Middle Ages 16). Turnhout 2020, pp. 115–136.

# About the Author

JEFFREY F. HAMBURGER, born in 1957 in London. BA in 1979 in English Literature and Art History, PhD in 1987 in Art History, Yale University, New Haven, "The Rothschild Canticles: Art and Mysticism in Flanders and the Rhineland ca. 1300," published by Yale University Press in 1990. Oberlin College, 1987–1997, from c. 1992 as Irving E. Houck Professor in the Humanities; the University of Toronto, 1997–2000; Harvard University, Department of the History of Art & Architecture, from 2000, since 2008 as the Kuno Francke Professor of German Art & Culture. Visiting professorships: École des Hautes Études (1997 & 2012), University of Zürich (2003 & 2005), University of Notre Dame (2005), Aston Visiting Lectureship, Oxford University (2008), Wolfgang Stammler Gastprofesseur, University of Fribourg (2010), Senior Visiting Fellow, Warburg Institute, London (2012), University of Hamburg (2014), Lectio Chair, University of Leuven (2014). Honors: Fulbright Fellowship, United Kingdom, Courtauld Institute (1979). Belgian-American Educational Foundation, Honorary Fellowship (1983). Gustave O. Arlt Award in the Humanities (1991). National Endowment for the Humanities Fellowship (1993 & 2016). Institute of Advanced Study, School of Historical Studies, Princeton, NJ (1993). John Nicholas Brown Prize, Medieval Academy of America (1994). Alexander von Humboldt-Stiftung Research Fellowship (1996 & 2006). Guggenheim Fellowship (1997). Jacques Barzun Prize in Cultural History, American Philosophical Society (1998). Otto Gründler Prize, International Congress of Medieval Studies (1999). Roland H. Bainton Book Prize in Art & Music, Sixteenth-Century Studies Conference (1999). Charles Rufus Morey Prize, College Art Association (1999). Fellow of the Medieval Academy of America (2001). Member of the American Academy of Arts & Sciences (2009). Mellor Prize, American Museum for Women in the Arts (2010). Member, American Philosophical Society (2010). Honorary Degree, University of Bern (2013). Anneliese Maier Research Prize, Humboldt Foundation (2015–2020). Bross Lectures, University of Chicago (2015). Corresponding Fellow, Monumenta Germaniae Historica (2016). Dumbarton Oaks, Visiting Scholar (2015–2016). Kress-Beinecke Professorship, Center for Advanced Study in the Visual Arts, National Gallery of Art, Washington, DC (2019–2020). Corresponding Member, Akademie der Wissenschaften zu Göttingen (2022). Gutenberg Prize of the International Gutenberg Society and the City of Mainz (2022). Panizzi Lectures, British Library (2022). International Center of Medieval Art, The Cloisters, Advisory Board (1995–1998). College Art Association, Art Bulletin, Advisory Board (1995–1998). Paris, Bibliothèque Nationale, Conseil scientifique for Catalogue of German Illuminated Manuscripts (1995–2004). Res: Anthropology and Aesthetics, Contributing Editor, from 1999. National Committee for the History of Art (2001–2004). Advisory Board, Katalog der deutschsprachigen illustrierten Handschriften des Mittelalters, Bayerische Akademie der Wissenschaften (since 2001). Centre de Recherches en Histoire de l'Art pour l'Europe du Nord – ARTES – de l'Université de Lille 3, Advisory Board (2001–2003). Centre International de Codicologie, Bibliothèque Royale Albert Ier, Brussels (since 2001). Kulturtopographie des alemannischen Raums: Texte und Untersuchungen (since 2009). Deutschen Handschriftenzentren, Advisory Board (2006). Medieval Women: Texts and Contexts Board Member (2010–2020). Zeitschrift für Kunstgeschichte, Editorial Board (2015–2019). Zeitschrift für deutsches Altertum und deutsche Philologie, Advisory Board (since 2011). Image – Text – Context, Editor, Pontifical Institute of Mediaeval Studies, Toronto (since 2012). Pierpont Morgan Library & Museum, Department of Manuscripts, Advisory Board (since 2015). Umění, Editorial Board (since 2016). John Rylands Research Institute Advisory Board (since 2017). Fitzwilliam Museum, Cambridge University, Research Advisory Group (since 2023).

**Research Interests:** Medieval art, especially illuminated manuscripts as well as interrelationships among art, piety, mysticism, and theology; text-image issues across various media; history of female monasticism; history of diagrams.

**Recent Publications:** (with Barbara Newman) *The Rothschild Canticles: Facsimile with Commentary*, Luzern, 2026. – *The Areopagite Through the Ages: A Millennium of Diagramming the Pseudo-Dionysius*, Toronto, 2026. – (with Beatrice Kitzinger & Joshua O'Driscoll) *Power, Patronage and Production: Book Arts from Central Europe (ca. 800–1500) in American Collections*, Toronto, 2026. – *The Diagram, Res: Anthropology and Aesthetics* 81–82, 2024. (with Eva Schlotheuber & Christina Jackel) *Wir Schwestern: Die vergessenen Chorfrauen von Klosterneuburg*, Jahresaustellung, Vienna, 2024. – (with Eva Schlotheuber) *The Ladies on the Hill: The Female Monastic Communities at the Aristocratic Monasteries of Klosterneuburg and St. George's in Prague*, Vienna, 2024. – *Flesh and Fabric: The Raiment of the Passion in a Crucifixion by Pietro Lorenzetti*, Florence, 2024. – (with David Roxburgh & Linda Safran) *The Diagram as Paradigm: Medieval Diagrams in a Cross-Cultural Perspective (Byzantine, Western European, and Islamicate)*, Washington, DC, 2022. – *Color in Cusanus*, Stuttgart, 2021. – *The Birth of the Author: Pictorial Prefaces in Glossed Books of the Twelfth Century*, Toronto, 2021. – (with Joshua O'Driscoll) *Imperial Splendor: The Art of the Book in the Holy Roman Empire,*

*800–1500*, New York, 2021. – *Kaiserliche Pracht: Deutsche Buchkunst von 800 bis 1500*, Luzern, 2021. – (with William Stoneman et al.) *Beyond Words: New Research on Illuminated Manuscripts in Boston Collections*, Toronto, 2021. – *Diagramming Devotion: Berthold of Nuremberg's Transformation of Hrabanus Maurus's Poems in Praise of the Cross*, Chicago, 2020. – (with Eva Schlotheuber) *The Liber ordinarius of Nivelles: Liturgy as Interdisciplinary Intersection*, with Eva Schlotheuber, Tübingen, 2019. (with Robert Suckale & Gude Sucakle Reflefsen) *Painting the Page in the Age of Print: Central European Manuscript Illumination of the Fifteenth Century*, Toronto, 2018. – (with Maria Theisen) *Unter Druck. Mitteleuropäische Buchmalerei im 15. Jahrhundert. Akten der Tagung, Wien, Österreichische Akademie der Wissenschaften, 13.1.–17.1.2016*, Petersberg, 2018. – (with Eva Schlotheuber et al.) *Liturgical Life and Latin Learning at Paradies bei Soest, 1300–1425*, Münster, 2017. – (with Brigitte Bedos-Rezak) *Sign and Design: Script as Image in a Cross-Cultural Perspective (300–1600 CE)*, Washington DC, 2016. – (with Nigel Palmer) *The Prayer Book of Ursula Begerin*, Dietikon, 2015. – (with Christoph Mackert) *10 Stationen zur mitteleuropäischen Buchmalerei des 15. Jahrhunderts*, Luzern, 2015. – *Script as Image*, Leuven, 2014.

Schwabe Verlag's signet was Johannes Petri's printer's mark. His printing workshop was established in Basel in 1488 and was the origin of today's Schwabe Verlag. The signet refers back to the beginnings of the printing press, and originated in the entourage of Hans Holbein. It illustrates a verse of Jeremiah 23:29: 'Is not my word like fire, says the Lord, and like a hammer that breaks a rock in pieces?'